My Thai book

Angsiyanan Ounping

Learn Thai

My Thai book

Author: Angsiyanan Ounping
&Thomas John Bowden

Publised by : Thaigomaster

E mail: thaigo59-master@yahoo.co.jp

Do you know

what a foreign accent is?

It's a sign of BRAVERY

Contents

Introduction

I have been teaching Thai for several years now and, at least most of the time, I love it. Thomas has been living in Thailand and studying Thai for the past 4 years. I love to talk to my students in my language and I feel incredibly proud when they try to learn my language. In comparison with many other languages, informal spoken Thai is uncomplicated; There are no tenses. Verb or noun inflections, agreements between nouns and verbs or nouns and adjectives, cases, genders or even articles. However, Thai is a tonal language, and tone is very important.
Central Thai, also known as Standard Thai or Siamese is the national and official language of Thailand, spoken by more than 65 million people or by almost 100 percent of the population. Spoken Thai is mutually intelligible with Laotian, the language of Laos; the two languages are linguistically very similar. Along with the numerous regional dialects, there are also several other ways of speaking the Thai language:

- Spoken Thai or street Thai – the informal way of speaking without polite terms of address. Usually used between close friends and relatives, this has become more and more common even outside of those circles in the modern age.
- Written Thai or elegant Thai – the formal way of speaking which uses polite terms. A simplified version of this is used in newspapers.
- Rhetorical Thai – primarily used for public speeches.
- Religious Thai – used when addressing monks or talking about Buddhism.
- Royal Thai – as you might have guessed thesis for addressing or talking about the royal family.

Acknowledgments
The author would like to thank the following people for their help in writing this book. Thaigomaster and his friend for being supportive of me and this project. Thomas John Bowden who provided input from a foreigner point of view. Leo Wang for his drawings and all my many students that sparked the ideas that make up much of the content of this book. Also, my family who are always beside me. This book would not have existed in the first place without any of you.
Angsiyanan OunpingAngsiyanan

The Thai writing

The Thai alphabet uses forty-four consonants, thirty-two vowels, four tone marks and various other symbols for punctuation. These are horizontally placed, left to right, with no intervening space, to form syllables, words and sentences. Vowels are written above, below, before, or after the consonant they modify, although the consonant always sounds first when the syllables are spoken. The vowel characters (and a few consonants) can be combined in various ways to produce numerous compound vowels.

Thai is generally phonetic. It is pronounced the way it is written. The alphabet also has 5 tones to learn: low, mid, high, falling, rising. The 'mid' tone has no tone mark, so essentially there are 4 to identify.

Thai is a tonal language. The tones correlate with the vowels and indicated in the script by a combination of the class of the initial consonant (high, mid or low), vowel length (long or short), closing consonant (dead or live) and, if indicated, one of four tone marks.

Learning to read and write Thai from the beginning has many advantages. Due to the fact that it is phonetic, you will be reinforcing your listening and speaking skill while learning to read and write. In fact, most people find that their pronunciation is more accurate when reading Thai script, it incorporates all the elements of pronunciation- including tones and vowel length.

ก ข ฃ ค ฅ ฆ ง จ ฉ
ช ซ ฌ ญ ฎ ฏ ฐ ฑ ฒ
ณ ด ต ถ ท ธ น บ ป
ผ ฝ ฟ ภ ม ร ล ว
ษ ส ห ฬ อ ฮ

Thai consonants (Sound / Phonetic Symbols)

There are 44 consonant characters in Thai and representing 20 consonant sounds.

Thai alphabet	Phonetic Symbols	Sounds like
ก	g	Go, Ski
ข ฃ ค ฅ ฆ	k	Kind, Kid
ด ฎ	d	Do
ต ฏ	dt	Stop, Stamp
ท ฑ ฒ ธ ถ ฐ	t	Teach
บ	b	Boy
ป	bp	Spot
พ ภ ผ	p	Pin
จ	j	Jet

ฉ ช ฌ	ch	Chat
ฟ ฝ	f	Fun
ซ ศ ษ ส	s	Sun, Sand
ย ญ	y	You
ว	w	Win
ห ฮ	h	Hand
ร	r	Rat
ล ฬ	l	Let
ม	m	Man
น ณ	n	Nine, Name
ง	ng	Ringing
อ	ɔɔ	Up, Egg

Some different consonants

dt as in stop — Bite your tongue.

bp as in spot — Explode your mouth.

g as in go — As in "goal"

ng as in ringing — It's from the back of your throat and nose.

Vowel phonetic symbols

There are short and long vowels which have the same pronunciation but with different lengths.

short	long	sound like
ɑ	ɑɑ	Far- Baht
ɔ	ɔɔ	Pot - Cause
o	oo	Go - Tone
u	uu	Book - Too
i	ii	Did - Deed
ʉ	ʉʉ	* like **U** with a smile
e	ee	Bet - Taste
ae	<u>ae</u>	Fat - Can
ə	əə	Modern - Dirt

Vowel combinations (Diphthongs)

Diphthongs	Sound like
ia	Beer
ʉa	Same as ia but the sound is from the throat
ua	Tour
am	Bun
ai	Hi
ao	Sound

Tones

Thai has 5 tones: mid, low, falling, high and rising tone. Tone marks will be put on top of words. If the tone changes the meaning changes too.

As in Thai language, we have 44 alphabets plus 22 vowels and 5 tones. To form a single word, you need to combine alphabet+vowel+tone.

Tone mark

Mid	Low	Falling	High	Rising
No mark	`	^	´	ˇ

Mid
The flat tone or the middle tone. This one stays flat throughout. Sometimes it drops down at the end a little bit.

Low
This tone is low and quite strong.

Falling
Starts high and comes down.

High
Tone starts high and keeps going up.

Rising
Starts low or mid and comes up at the end.

TONE SHAPE AND APPROXIMATE FREQUENCY

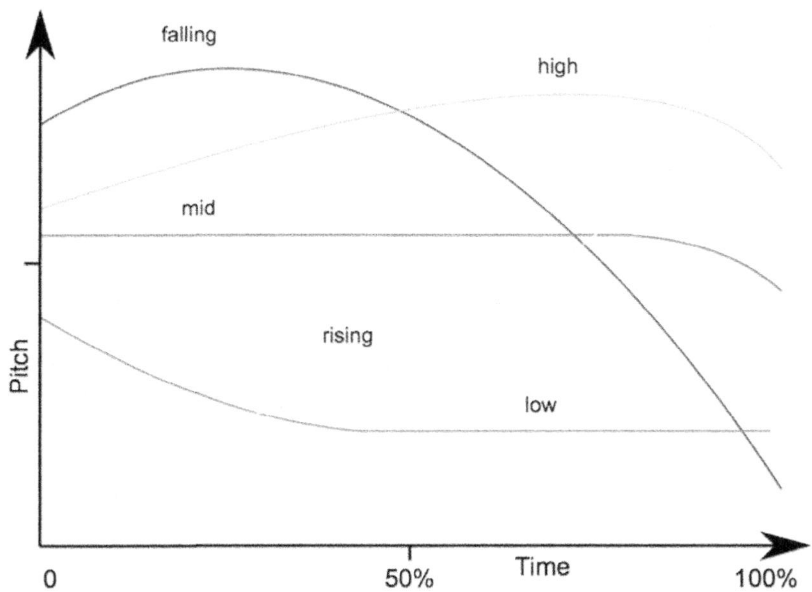

Trick to remember and pronounce each tone correctly

TONE

Mid	Low	Falling	High	Rising
-	ˋ	^	ˊ	ˇ
normal and flat	Angry	Tired	Lady	Song

Mid: Normal and flat. Keep in mind English is anything but normal and flat. You are going for emotionless here.

Low: A low is more like you are grumpy or angry about something. You don't have to snarl but you should sound as though you are particularly annoyed with that **kàao** ข่าว (news)

Falling: As the name implies a falling tone shoots up and then drops back down. Don't have a **kâao** ข้าว (rice) man.

High: A high tone starts high and then goes even higher. It does not drop back down. Think of a high-pitched woman's voice. You wanna go **mái** มั้ย (Question word)

Rising: A rising tone is like singing a song; You drop down to a low tone and then come right back up to a high tone. If you are trying to compliment a beautiful woman make sure you say **sŭai** สวย (Beautiful) with a smooth rising tone. If you were to say it with a mid tone **suai** ซวย (bad luck) you would be telling her she has bad luck or is an unfortunate person.

Remember: Different tone = completely different meaning.

Example

Mid	Low	Falling	High	Rising
-	`	^	´	ˇ
mai	mài	mâi	mái	mǎi
-	new	no	question word	question word

Practice the following words

Mid ↔ Normal

gin	To eat
maa	To come
duu	To look
dii	Good
dtaa	Eyes

Low ↔ Angry

gài	Chicken
jà	Will
gàp	With
sài	Put in
pèt	Spicy

Falling ⟷ Tired

mâi	No
chɔ̂ɔp	Like
bâan	House
mâe	Mum
pɔ̂ɔ	Dad

High ⟷ Lady

mái	Question word
máa	Horse
náam	Water
rɔ́ɔn	Hot
lék	Small

Rising ⟷ Song

mǎa	Dog
sǔai	Beautiful
mǔu	Pig/pork
hǐw	Hungry
kǎa	Legs

Question words

Question	Meaning	Example sentense
à-rai?	What?	kun gin **à-rai?**
tîi-nǎi	Where?	kun yàak bpai **tîi-nǎi?**
mʉ̂a-rai	When?	kun glàp America **mʉ̂a-rai?**
yàang rai/ yang ngai	How?	kun maa tîi-nîi **yàng rai/yang ngai?**
rʉ́-yang?	Have...yet?	kun gin kâao **rʉ́-yang?**
nǎi	Classifier+ nǎi (Which)?	kon **nǎi?** an **nǎi?**
krai	Who?	**krai** pûut paa-sǎa Thai dâi?
tam-mai	Why?	**tam-mai** kun mâi chɔ̂ɔp bpai tá-lee?
gìi	How much/How many?	kun rian Thai **gìi** wan?

Note: Usually we put question words at the end of a sentence. Two notable exceptions are **krai** (who) and **tam-mai** (why) which are placed at the beginning of the sentence.

Example sentense

kun gin à-rai? — What do you eat?

tam-mai kun mâi chɔ̂ɔp bpai tá-lee? — Why don't you like going to the ocean?

kun yàak bpai tîi-nǎi? — Where would you like to go?

krai pûut paa-sǎa Thai dâi? — Who can speak Thai?

Kun jà glàp America mʉ̂a-rai? — When will you go back to America?

kun maa tîi-nîi yàng-rai/yang-ngai? — How did you get here?
kon nǎi? — Which person?
an nǎi? — Which one?
kun gin kâao rʉ́-yang? — Have you eaten yet?
kun rian Thai gìi wan? — How many days do you study Thai? (per week)

Shocking Questions

Most questions you will be asked are normal small talk but sometimes you might feel surprised by these oddly specific questions. Where exactly have you been today, Neighbour?
Common examples:

Kun bpai tîi-nǎi? — Where are you going?
Kun bpai tîi-nǎi maa — Where have you been?
kun gin kâao rʉ́-yang? — Have you eaten yet?

In truth, these are just a type of greeting and they do not demand a detailed response.

kun dtaeng-ngaan rʉ́-yang? — Have you married yet?
kun ngən dʉan tâo-rài? — How much is your salary?
Tam-mai lə̂ək gàp káo? — Why did you break up with him?

These are normal questions in Thailand and are not considered nosy.

LESSON 1

Greeting

Culturamnl differences;

In Thailand, we have a strong culture and tradition regarding age and status, particularly towards the elderly. Young people must show respect to their elders. That's why when we greet somebody who is older than us (or of a higher social status) we try to be very polite and we will 'WAI' as a sign of respect.

"Wai" is the act of putting your hands together in front of you, as though in prayer. The position of the hands from lower (in front of your neck) to higher (in front of your face) signify just how much respect you are showing. You don't need to go overboard for a simple greeting but this is useful to know.
The Wai can mean;
"Hello," "Thank you," "I'm sorry" or "Goodbye".

When somebody Wais you, you should return the Wai to show respect and acknowledgement.
A Wai is not used to greet children, servants, street vendors or laborers. Also, we don't return a wai to a child, waiter or clerk. A simple smile is sufficient.

Thai people **do** Wai for a Monk even if that monk is younger than them or is a child but monks will not return the Wai. Don't think they are being rude if they do not return your Wai.

Touching one another in public is generally frowned upon in Thai culture Shaking hands or even hugging is common in western culture but can be quite jarring for a Thai person. Boys and Girls touching is a particularly interesting point; in the past, the simple act of touching could mean you are suddenly engaged to be married!

Thais are mostly Buddhist and this brings further weight to the importance of different parts of the body. The head is the highest part and thus considered 'clean' Touching somebodies head is a no-no. On the flip-side the feet are the lowest and 'dirtiest' part of the body. While for foreigners it is common to kick your feet up on a table/chair when relaxing, this is considered quite rude in Thailand. More importantly you should avoid using your feet to point at things and **never** point at a person with your feet. That cool thing in the market you were pointing at to get a discount on? That price will now be set in stone because you insulted the shop owner.

Polite words;

There are two common words in Thai that show respect and make a sentence more polite. They are used at the end of a sentence. *kâ* for women and *krâp* for men (sometime pronounce *cup*) and is also used for statements, commands and to respond "YES" and "Thank you"

- The word *kâ (for women) use in any situation.*
- The word *ká (for women) use at the end of question*
- The word *krâp (for men) use in any situation.*

Pronouns

kun	chăn	pŏm	káo	rao	man
You	I (for women)	I (for men)	He/She They/Them	We	It
คุณ	ฉัน	ผม	เขา	เรา	มัน

What's your name?

à-rai?
What
อะไร

chʉ̂ʉ	chʉ̂ʉ lên	chʉ̂ʉ jing
Name	Nick name	Given name
ชื่อ	ชื่อเล่น	ชื่อจริง

PATTERN PRACTICE

What's your name?

kun káo	chʉ̂ʉ	à-rai?

My name is ...

chăn	chʉ̂ʉ Ang kâ
pŏm	chʉ̂ʉ Tom kráp

Title and name
The word kun, which means you, can also be used for the title of women and men
Kun Ang, Kun Peter

Thai nicknames
Thai nicknames can be very funny for foreigners because literally everything in the world can be a nickname for a Thai person. The plus side is you can pick up new vocabulary from these strange names. So, make some new friends and ask them what their name means.

My name is sôm (orange)
My name is kâao (rice)
My name is bpépsîi (Pepsi)
My name is náam (water)
My name is dtaeng-mo (watermelon)

where are you from?

maa	jàak	tîi-nǎi
Come	From	Where
มา	จาก	ที่ไหน

bprà-têt	mʉang	rát	jang-wàt
Country	City	State	Province
ประเทศ	เมือง	รัฐ	จังหวัด

PATTERN PARTICE

What country are you from?

kun káo kun Dave	maa-jàak	bprà-têt mʉang rát jang-wàt	à-rai?

I'm from.....

chăn		bprà-tɵ̂t.......
pŏm	maa-jàak	mʉang........
kun Dave		rát ....
		jang-wàt.....

Countries

à-meɵ-ri-gaa	ɔ́ɔt-sà-dtrɵ-	Ang-grìt	Fáràng-sɵ̀et	Yəə-rà-man
America	ria Australia	England	France	Germany
อเมริกา	ออสเตรเรีย	อังกฤษ	ฝรั่งเศส	เยอรมัน

Yîi-bpùn	Gao-lĭi	Jiin	Pá-mâa	Laaw
Japan	Korea	China	Myanmar	Laos
ญี่ปุ่น	เกาหลี	จีน	พม่า	ลาว

Nationality

Have you ever heard the word **fà-ràng?**

It's a word used by Thai people to describe Caucasians. Derived from the word for the French people who came during the time of the French Indochina. It is not used for Asian people. Instead we will put 'kon" which just means "people" in front of their nationality. Such as:

kon jiin (Chinese), kon yîi-bpùn (Japanese), kon gao-lĭi (Korean)

You could also say "American" as kon à-mee-rì-gaa

How are you?

mái?
Question word
ไหม

sàbaai-dii	mâi sàbaai	chǎi chǎi
Fine	Not well	So so
สบายดี	ไม่สบาย	เฉย เฉย

PATTERN PARTICE

How are you?

kun káo kun Tom	sàbaai-dii	mái?

I'm fine / I'm not well

chán pǒm káo kun Tom	sàbaai-dii mâi sàbaai

Thai people don't always say **sàbaai-dii mái.**
gin kâao rʉ́-yang? (have you eaten yet?) is another common question you will hear.
We use this frequently because when you ask gin kâao rʉ́-yang?
It shows you care about this person and are interested in their day, even if it is just small talk.

YES/NO QUESTION

To make simple questions put (mái) after the word. Mái can also be used for invitations or suggestions.

Most common words

rɔ́ɔn	kâo-jai	sà-nùk	sǔai	à-rɔ̀ɔi	pèt	hǐw
Hot	Understand	Fun	Beautiful	Delicious	Spicy	Hungry
ร้อน	เข้าใจ	สนุก	สวย	อร่อย	เผ็ด	หิว

Yes/No

châi	mâi
Yes	No
ใช่	ไม่

Like/Don't like

chɔ̂ɔp	mâi chɔ̂ɔp
Like	Don't like
ชอบ	ไม่ชอบ

Very/A little bit

mâak	nít-nɔ̀ɔi	yə́
Very/a lot (for feeling)	A little bit	A lot (for noun)
มาก	นิดหน่อย	เยอะ

Easy way to create sentences

In Thai we don't really use different words to show time tense. The way to represent tense is to mention the time, day or date at the beginning of a sentence to show when that situation happened.

Time	Subject	Verb	Obj/Adv/Adj	Question
	Thailand		sǔai	mái?
	kun	chɔ̂ɔp		mái?
	pizza		pèt	mái?
wan-níi (today)	kun	sà-nùk		mái?

Translate

mʉang thai sǔai mái?	Is Thailand beautiful?
kun chɔ̂ɔp mái?	Do you like...?
pizza pèt mái?	Is (that) pizza spicy?
wan-níi kun sà-nùk mái?	Are you having fun today?

PATTERN PRACTICE

Are/is..? Do/does...?

kun káo	chɔ̂ɔp kâo-jai hǐw	mái?

Answering

To answer "yes" simply repeat the verb or adjective and to say "no" just put mâi before the verb or adjective.

chăn pŏm káo	chɔ̂ɔp kâo-jai hǐw mâi chɔ̂ɔp mâi kâo-jai mâi hǐw	mâak nít-nɔ̀ɔi

Goodbye /Good luck

The formal way to say goodbye is the same as hello. **sà wàt dii**

Informal way

- bpai gɔ̀ɔn ná — I'm going
- glàp gɔ̀ɔn ná — I'm going back

Another way to say goodbye for situations where you won't be seeing each other for a long time.

- Laa-gɔ̀ɔn — Goodbye

See you again

póp/jəə	gan	mài
To meet	Each other	New/Anew/Again
พบ/เจอ	กัน	ใหม่

Two ways to say

- póp gan mài — See you again
- jəə gan mài — See you again

Good luck

Saying good luck is very common in Thai. You can use it in every situation imaginable.

chôok	dii
Luck	Good
โชค	ดี

- chôok-dii — Good luck

Useful expressions

What did you say? / Pardon?	à-rai ná?
Excuse me/ Sorry	kɔ̌ɔ-tôot
That's all right/ It doesn't matter	mâi-bpən-rai
No problem	mâi mii bpan-hǎa
Yes, that's right	châi
No, that's wrong	mâi châi
Oh? / Really?	Jing-rɔ̌ɔ
Really/It's true!	jing jing
No worries / Everything is as it should be	sàbaai sàbaai
And you?	kun là
Nice to meet you	yin-dii-tîi-dâi-rúu-jàk

Thai people always say "**greng jai**" เกรงใจ
While this expression does not have a direct equivalent in English it literally means "to be afraid of offending." Thai people usually use this when they feel it is rude to ask for something or if they are offered something they feel is excessive. That person will feel "greng jai" and usually turn down the offer or not ask for a favour.

Note:
If you really want to give something to a Thai person you should offer it 3 times. They will usually accept on the third attempt.

Exercise

1. ___kun sǔai mâak
2. ___kun kâo-jai mái?
3. ___kun chʉ̂ʉ à-rai?
4. ___chán/pǒm maa jàak bprà-tɵ̂t Thai
5. ___káo chʉ̂ʉ.....
6. ___kun maa-jàak tîi-nǎi?
7. ___chôok-dii
8. ___kun sàbaai dii mái?
9. ___mâi bpɵn rai

A. Good luck

B. I'm from Thailand

C. You are so beautiful

D. What is your name?

E. Where are you from?

F. His/She name is...

G. Do you understand?

H. It doesn't matter/ That's all right

I. How are you?

Conversation

Ang: Sàwàtdii kâ

Tom: Sàwàtdii Kráp

Ang: Kun chʉ̂ʉ àrai ká?

Tom: pǒm chʉ̂ʉ Tom Kráp, Kun là?

Ang: Chán chʉ̂ʉ. Ang kâ

Kun sàbaai dii mái ká?

Tom: pǒm sàbaai dii Kráp, Kun là?

Ang: Chán mâi sàbaai kâ.

Ang: Kun maa Jàak bprà-têt àrai ká?

Tom: pǒm maa Jàak bprà-têt Australia Kráp

Australia rɔ́ɔn mâak

Kun Ang maa Jàak mʉang àrai Kráp?

Ang: Chán maa Jàak Chiangmai kâ.

Tom: Chiangmai sǔai mái?

Ang: Chiangmai sǔai mâak kâ, Chiangmai mii Fáràng yə

Tom: Oh, jing-rɔ̌ɔ pǒm chɔ̂ɔp Chiangmai Kráp

Ang: Yin dii tîi dâi rúu jàk kâ

Tom: Yin dii tîi dâi rúu jàk Kráp

LESSON 2

Place ___________

In Thailand, there are many interesting places to visit. Every part of Thailand has a unique culture, local dialect, style of food, lifestyle and even plantlife.

When at the temple (wat) you should try to be careful about your actions and clothing; do not wear short or sexy clothes and remember to show respect. Most temples have signs to let you know what is and is not acceptable.

Cinema (rong nang). If you have the chance to go to a cinema in Thailand you might be surprised when the movie starts. The royal anthem will play with various clips of the King and everyone will stand. When in Rome do as the Romans do.

When asking for directions in Thailand don't be surprised when the directions you receive are completely wrong. Thai people always want to be kind and helpful but this can result in an inability to directly refuse or say "I don't know." They really want to help even when they don't understand your language or what you're asking. Sometimes you can ask 3 Thai people and you will receive 3 different answers. Even though you never get good directions just remember they have good intentions.

I want to go

yàak	bpai	bpai-tîaw
Want to	Go	Take a trip
อยาก	ไป	ไปเที่ยว

hɔ̂ɔng-náam	ráan-aahǎan	tá-naa-kaan	dtà-làat	sà-nǎam-bin
Toilet	Restaurant	Bank	Market	Airport
ห้องน้ำ	ร้านอาหาร	ธนาคาร	ตลาด	สนามบิน

rong-pá-yaa- baan	Rong-rian	bâan	hâang	sà-tǎa-nii dtam-rùat
Hospital	School	House	Shopping mall	Police station
โรงพยาบาล	โรงเรียน	บ้าน	ห้าง	สถานีตำรวจ

PATTERN PRACTICE

I want to go

chǎn pǒm káo	yàak	bpai bpai-tîaw	dtà-làat hâang sà-nǎam-bin

The word **bpai** means "go" and can be used for any situation where you go somewhere.

Bpai tîaw is used for taking a trip or long vacation. You can also use it when you are just going somewhere for fun even if that place is not far away. Such as the Market, Shopping mall or Amusement park.

where is..?

tîi-năi	yùu
Where	To be at a place To live / To stay
ที่ไหน	อยู่

PATTERN PRACTICE

where is..?

hɔ̂ɔng-náam ráan-aahăan tá-naa-kaan	yùu	tîi-năi?

The word "where" **tîi-năi?** can be shortened to just **"năi?"**. So you can ask **yùu năi?**

where is..?

dtà-làat sà-năam-bin rong-pá-yaa-baan	yùu năi?

Location

tîi-nîi	tîi-nân	tîi-nôon
Here	There	Over there
ที่นี่	ที่นั่น	ที่โน่น

Place located........

Rong-rian	yùu	tîi-nîi
bâan		tîi-nân
hâang		tîi-nôon
sà-tăa-nii dtam-		

The word **yùu**
You will never forget **yùu** when talking about location. It always comes after the subject.
Question: **Subject+ yùu+ tîi-năi?**
Answer: **Subject+ yùu+ preposition+position/location**

How to use proper syntax.

Place + name

wát Prá gâew	Temple of the Emerald buddha
Rong-pá-yaa-baan Sirirâat	Siriraj Piyamaharajkarun Hospital
mà-hăa-wít-tá-yaa-lai Oxford	Oxford university
mà-hăa-wít-tá-yaa-lai Cambridge	Cambridge university

Preposition of place

glâi Near ใกล้	glai Far ไกล

dtrong-bpai Go straight ตรงไป	líaw-sáai Turn left เลี้ยวซ้าย	líaw-kwǎa Turn right เลี้ยวขวา	dtrong-kâam Opposite ตรงข้าม

rá-wàng In-between ระหว่าง	dtìt-gàp Next to ติดกับ	tîi At ที่	tǎew Around (area) แถว

PATTERN PRACTICE

hɔ̂ɔng	yùu	glâi	dtà-làat
náam		glai	hɔ̂ɔng-náam
dtà-làat		dtrong-kâam	ráan-aahǎan
bâan		rá-wàang	ta-naa-kaan
hâang		dtìt-gàp	
		tîi	

Places vocabulary

ráan - shop

ráan aahǎan (shop food) Restaurant **ร้านอาหาร**	ráan nǎng-sʉ̌ʉ (shop book) Book store **ร้านหนังสือ**	ráan gaa-fae (shop coffee) Coffee shop **ร้านกาแฟ**
ráan kǎai yaa (shop sell medicine) Pharmacy **ร้านขายยา**	ráan dtàt pǒm (shop cut hair) Baber shop **ร้านตัดผม**	ráan sɔ̂ɔm computer (shop fix computer) Computer repair shop **ร้านซ่อมคอมพิวเตอร์**

Rong-big building

Rong rian (big building for study) School **โรงเรียน**	rong nǎng (big building for movie) Cinema **โรงหนัง**	rong pá-yaa-baan (big building for nursing) Hospital **โรงพยาบาล**
rong raem (big building for stay) Hotel **โรงแรม**	rong aahǎan (big building for food) Canteen/ Cafeteria **โรงอาหาร**	rong ngaan (big building for work) Factory **โรงงาน**

sà-năam - Field

sà-năam bin (Field for flying) Airport สนามบิน	sà-năam gii-laa (Field for sport) Stadium สนามกีฬา	sà-năam gɔɔp (Field for golf) Golf course สนามกอล์ฟ
sà-năam fút- bɔɔn (Field for football) Football field สนามฟุตบอล	sà-năam dèk lên (Field for kids to play) Playground สนามเด็กเล่น	sà-năam yâa (Field for grass) Yard สนามหญ้า

sà-tăa-nii – station

sà-tăa-nii rót-bát (station for bus) Bus station สถานีรถบัส	sà-tăa-nii kŏn-sòng (station for transpotation) Bus station สถานีขนส่ง	sà-tăa-nii rót-fai (station for train) Train station สถานีรถไฟ
sà-tăa-nii dtam-rùat (station for police) Police station สถานีตำรวจ	sà-tăa-nii dàp pləəng (station for stop fire) Fire station สถานีดับเพลิง	sà-tăa-nii a-naa-mai (station for health) Public health centre สถานีอนามัย

hɔ̂ɔng - room

hɔ̂ɔng-náam Restroom ห้องน้ำ	hɔ̂ɔng-sàmùt Library ห้องสมุด	hɔ̂ɔng-nɔɔn Bedroom ห้องนอน
hɔ̂ɔng-tam-ngaan Working room ห้องทำงาน	hɔ̂ɔng-rian Study room ห้องเรียน	hɔ̂ɔng-krua Kitchen ห้องครัว

Attractions places

tá-lee Ocean ทะเล	bprai-sà-nii Post office ไปรษณีย์	sà-tǎan-tûut Embassy สถานทูต	dtɔɔ-mɔɔ Immigration ตรวจคนเข้าเมือง
wát Temple วัด	bpàa Forest ป่า	náam dtòk Waterfall น้ำตก	puu-kǎo/dɔɔi Mountain ภูเขา/ดอย

Vocabulary

bpám náam-man	Gas station	ปั๊มน้ำมัน
sǔan	Garden	สวน
sǔan-sàt	Zoo	สวนสัตว์
suǎn sǎa-taa-rà-ná	Public garden	สวนสาธารณะ
bòot	Church	โบสถ์
ráan-sàdùak-sʉ́ʉ	Covenience store	ร้านสะดวกซื้อ
pí-pít-tà-pan	Museum	พิพิธภัณฑ์
yim	Gym	ยิม
sà-wâai-náam	Swimming pool	สระว่ายน้ำ
laan-jɔ̀ɔt-rót	Car park	ลานจอดรถ
tà-nǒn	Road	ถนน
sɔɔi	Alley	ซอย
sà-paan	Bridge	สะพาน
fai-daeng	Traffic light	ไฟแดง

Past tense

To make a basic sentence in the past tense put the word "**maa**" which means come (not in this case) at the end.

Where have you been?

kun bpai tîi-năi **maa**? — Where have you been?

kun bpai năi **maa**? — Where have you been?

I have been to

chăn bpai Rong-rian **maa** — I went to school.

pŏm bpai dtà-làat **maa** — I went to the market.

káo bpai Rong-pá-yaa-baan **maa** — He went to hospital.

kun bpai năi?
kun bpai năi maa?
These two sentences can also be used as greetings.

Talking about places

Bpen-yang-ngai?
How is/was.....?
เป็นยังไง

tam-ma-châat	bɔɔ-ri-gaan	ban-yaa-gàat
Nature	Service	Atmosphere
ธรรมชาติ	บริการ	บรรยากาศ

suǎi	paeng	sà-àat	nâa-sǒn-jai	sà-nùk	sòk-gà-bpròk
Beautiful	Expensive	Clean	Interesting	Fun	Dirty
สวย	แพง	สะอาด	น่าสนใจ	สนุก	สกปรก

PATTERN PRACTICE

How is Chiangmai?

Chiangmai bpen-yang-ngai? — How is Chiangmai?

Chiangmai is...

Chiangmai		
	suǎi	Chiangmai is beautiful.
	paeng	Chiangmai is expensive.
	sà-àat	Chiangmai is clean.
	nâa-sǒn-jai	Chiangmai is interesting.
	sà-nùk	Chiangmai is fun.
	sòk-gà-bpròk	Chiangmai is dirty.
	sǐang-dang	Chiangmai is noisy.
	nâa-bʉa	Chiangmai is boring.

Possessive

kɔ̌ɔng

Belong to/of

ของ

Noun	Belong to/of	Noun	Meaning
mâe	kɔ̌ɔng	chán	My mum
faen	kɔ̌ɔng	pǒm	My girlfriend
pʉ̂an	kɔ̌ɔng	kun John	John's friend
bâan	kɔ̌ɔng	pǒm	My house

PATTERN PRACTICE

bâan kɔ̌ɔng chán	My house.
an-níi kɔ̌ɔng chán	This one is mine.
grà-bpǎo kɔ̌ɔng kun sǔai mâak	Your bag is very beautiful.
mâe kɔ̌ɔng pǒm yùu Australia	My mum lives in Australia.

Useful expressions

Excuse me/ Sorry	kɔ̌ɔ-tôot
Lost (I'm lost!)	lǒng-taang
Have a good trip	tîaw hâi sà-nùk
Have a safe trip	dəən taang bpɔ̀ɔt-pai
Could you help me?	chûai nɔ̀ɔi dâi mái?
Thank you	kɔ̀ɔp kun
Think that	kít-wâa
And	láe
And/And then	lá-gɔ̂ɔ
Have	mii
No	mâi
Interesting	nâa-sǒn-jai
Where are you going?	bpai nǎi?
Where have you been?	bpai nǎi maa?
Enjoy your trip	tîaw-hâi-sànùk ná
Go for a walk	dəən-lên

LESSON 3

Number

Numbers are very important to Thai people.

Since the day you were born the date and time of your birth could be used to predict your entire future. Most Thai people truly believe this.

Before naming your child a Thai monk or Mor duu (fortune teller) will check the childs date of birth and then give a name based off of this.

Maybe your parents will quietly show a fortune teller (Mor duu) you and your partners date of birth to check if you are a good match. Suddenly mum might not like your girlfriend anymore based on this prediction.

Numerology is very important in Thai culture. For example, the number 9 (gâo) is an auspicious number. In Thai Gâo means "step forward" or "progress."

The number 9 is used in many positive names that refer to Prosperity Future. So, the number '9' is also thought to be lucky in Thai culture. That's why Thai people will do events or activities Buddhism on 9th. And also, number of items with number 9 or end with number total 9.

Have you ever seen your Thai friends write "5555" in chat?

Number 5 in Thai pronounced hâa. So, when you see five-five-five that means we are laughing out loud. HA-HA-HA.

Thai people love the lottery. Following their love of numbers, Thai people naturally love buying lottery tickets. They will use numbers from anything that might seem important; From their dreams or meditations to the license plate of a car they were in an accident with.

Numbers

1	2	3	4	5	6	7	8	9	10
nʉ̀ng	sɔ̌ɔng	sǎam	sìi	hâa	hòk	jèd	bp<u>aè</u>t	gâo	sìp
หนึ่ง	สอง	สาม	สี่	ห้า	หก	เจ็ด	แปด	เก้า	สิบ

Multiples of 10 + 1 are an exception and will read ***èt***

11	12	13	14	15
sìp-èt	sìp-sɔ̌ɔng	sìp-sǎam	sìp-sìi	sìp- hâa
สิบเอ็ด	สิบสอง	สิบสาม	สิบสี่	สิบห้า

16	17	18	19	20
sìp-hòk	sìp-jèd	sìp-bp<u>aè</u>t	sìp-gâo	yîi-sìp
สิบหก	สิบเจ็ด	สิบแปด	สิบเก้า	ยี่สิบ

20 is an exception its **yîi sìp**

21	25	27	29	30
yîi-sìp èt	yîi-sìp hâa	yîi-sìp jèd	yîi-sìp gâo	sǎam-sìp
ยี่สิบเอ็ด	ยี่สิบห้า	ยี่สิบเจ็ด	ยี่สิบเก้า	สามสิบ

31	50	70	90	99
sǎam-sìp èt	hâa-sìp	jèt-sìp	gâo-sìp	gâo-sìp gâo
สามสิบเอ็ด	ห้าสิบ	เจ็ดสิบ	เก้าสิบ	เก้าสิบเก้า

100	(nʉ̀ng) **rɔ́ɔi**
1,000	(nʉ̀ng) **pan**
10,000	(nʉ̀ng) **mʉ̀ʉn**
100,000	(nʉ̀ng) **s<u>ǎe</u>n**
1,000,000	(nʉ̀ng) **láan**

Higher numbers aren't abbreviated like in English. Thai numbers are very verbose in comparison;
1,000 nʉ̀ng pan

1,300 nʉ̀ng pan sǎam rɔ́ɔi

5,356 hâa-pan sǎam-rɔ́ɔi hâa-sìp-hòk

3,872			
3	8	7	2
sǎam-pan (3,000)	bp<u>àe</u>d-rɔ́ɔi (800)	jèd-sìp (70)	sɔ̌ɔng (2)

50,000 hâa mʉ̀ʉn

34,500 sǎam mʉ̀ʉn sìi pan hâa rɔ́ɔi

55,953				
5	5	9	5	3
hâa-mʉ̀ʉn (50,000)	hâa-pan (5,000)	gâao-rɔ́ɔi (900)	hâa-sìp (50)	sǎam (3)

NOTE: This holds true for higher number too. 100,000, 100,000,000 etc.

Thai numerals

๑	๒	๓	๔	๕	๖	๗	๘	๙	๑๐
nʉ̀ng	sɔ̌ɔng	sǎam	sìi	hâa	hòk	jèd	bpaèt	gâo	sìp
หนึ่ง	สอง	สาม	สี่	ห้า	หก	เจ็ด	แปด	เก้า	สิบ

Thai price and Tourist price

Sometimes you will find there is a Thai price and a tourist price. This is somewhat common in museums and tourist attractions. Sometimes this price will be displayed "in the open" for all to see but usually the Thai price will be displayed in Thai numerals and the tourist price in English numerals. While the practice is technically against the Thai constitution it likely won't go away so long as people choose to support it.

Asking the price

gìi...... ? How many? กี่	tâo-rai How much/ How many? เท่าไร

an níi This one อันนี้	an nán That one อันนั้น	an nón That one (further away) อันโน้น

PATTERN PRACTICE

How much is this?

an níi an nán an nón	gìi	Baht ? Dollar? Yen? Won?
an níi an nán	tâo-rai?	

Telling the price or number

This........	an níi an nán	100 THB 10,000 yen 200 dollars

How are **gìi** and **tâo-rai** different?
tâo-rai can be used alone.
gìl must be followed by the classifier words. In Thai, we use classifiers for everything. English have classifiers also. but they are used much less frequently. If you went to the bakery would you ask for "2 breads"?
Example:

gìl baht — How many baht?
gìi wan — How many day?

How much per

an lá Each one is... อันละ

PATTERN PRACTICE

an lá tâo-rai?	How much per item?
an lá 20 Baht	20 Baht each.
sɔ̌ɔng an tâo-rai?	How much for 2?
sɔ̌ɔng an 100 Baht	100 baht for 2.

Haggling

As you might already know, Haggling is the norm when shopping in the markets, small shops or when you are buying in bulk. You don't need to haggle but the first price is rarely the best price. Department stores and upscale shops work the same way as western countries, meaning the price is usually fixed. Food vendors on the street also have set pricing. It's already very cheap and the prices are usually equal throughout the entire city.

paeng Expensive แพง	mâi paeng Not expensive ไม่แพง	tùuk Cheap ถูก

ao Want to take เอา	mâi ao Not take ไม่เอา

PATTERN PRACTICE

Q: ao mái?	Do you want it?
A: ao / mâi ao	Yes/No
Q: ao mái?	Would you like one?
A: mâi ao, paeng mâak	No, it's very expensive.
Q: ao gìi an?	How many do you want?
A: ao 2 an	I want 2 items (classifier)

dâi mái?
Can (you)?
ได้ไหม

dâi	mâi dâi
Can	Can not
ได้	ไม่ได้

lót	nɔ̀ɔi	sʉ́ʉ
Discount	Please	To buy
ลด	หน่อย	ซื้อ

PATTERN PRACTICE

Can you give me a discount?

Q: lót nɔ̀ɔi	dâi mái?	Can you discount?
300 THB	dâi mái?	How about 300 THB, ok?

Can/ Can not

A1: dâi — Can.

A2: mâi dâi — Can not.

Classifiers

This can be the most difficult part of Thai. Classifiers are not just used occasionally as in English. They are used for every single thing. There are over 600 classifiers in the Thai language.

What is a classifier?
English also has classifiers:

- A loaf of bread
- A bar of chocolate
- A bottle of water
- A piece of cake

But in Thai we have classifiers for every object and item. Classifiers are used when you want to count objects and each object has its own specific classifier.

Because we have so many classifiers to the point that even Thai people have trouble remembering them all we have some generic ones that are a bit more versatile. These 3 classifiers will see you through many situations:

- **an** - Can be roughly translate to "item" An 'an' is a general classifier that can be used to refer to any object. Try to use the correct classifier but remember you can always fall back on this one.
- **dtua** - Means "Body" and is used for animals, clothes and furniture.
- **kon** - Used for people only. It's better to not refer to people as objects.

an For things, Items อัน	dtua Animal/Clothes/Furniture ตัว	kon People คน

How to use classifiers

Numbers can only be placed **before** the classifier.

Noun	Number	Classifier	meaning
bpàak-gaa ปากกา	1	an อัน	1 pen
maew แมว	2	dtua ตัว	2 cats
pûu-chaai ผู้ชาย	3	kon คน	3 men

PATTERN PRACTICE

What do you want to buy?

ao à-rai?	What do you want to get?
sʉ́ʉ à-rai?	What do you want to buy?

I would like to buy...

	sʉ̂a		dtua	1 shirt .
ao	gaang-gəng		dtua	1 pair of pants.
	rɔɔng-táao	1	kûu	1 pair of shoes.
sʉ́ʉ	grà-bpǎo	2	bai	1 bag.
	sɔ̂ɔi-kɔɔ		sên	1 necklace.
	wâen-dtaa		an	1 pair of glasses.

Colour

sǐi Colour สี

ɔ̀ɔn Light อ่อน	kêm/gæ̀e Dark เข้ม/แก่

color	English	Thai
sǐi daeng	Red	สีแดง
sǐi dam	Black	สีดำ
sǐi lʉ̌ang	Yellow	สีเหลือง
sǐi chom-puu	Pink	สีชมพู
sǐi kǐaw	Green	สีเขียว
sǐi sôm	Orange	สีส้ม
sǐi kǎaw	White	สีขาว
sǐi fáa	Blue	สีฟ้า
sǐi náam-ngən	Dark blue	สีน้ำเงิน
sǐi náam-dtaan	Brown	สีน้ำตาล
sǐi mûang	Violet	สีม่วง
sǐi tao	Gray	สีเทา
sǐi tɔɔng	Gold	สีทอง
sǐi ngən	Silver	สีเงิน

Place the adjective after the noun

Noun + Adjective
Colour + ɔ̀ɔn/kêm/gàe

PATTERN PRACTICE

sʉ̂a sǐi-daeng	Red shirt.
grà-bpǎo sǐi-dam	Black bag.
rɔɔng-táo sǐi-chom-puu	Pink shoes.
too-rà-sàp sǐi-kǐaw ɔ̀ɔn	Light green telephone.

Exercise
Write the name of each colour underneath it

Vocabulary

sʉ̂a	Shirt	เสื้อ
gaang-gɵng	Pants	กางเกง
rɔɔng-táao	Shoes	รองเท้า
grà-bpǎo	Bag	กระเป๋า
grà-bprong	Skirt	กระโปรง
tǔng-táao	Sock	ถุงเท้า
sɔ̂ɔi-kɔɔ	Necklace	สร้อยคอ
wâen-dtaa	Glasses	แว่นตา
naa-li-gaa	Watch	นาฬิกา
mùak	Hat	หมวก
kɵ̌m-kàt	Belt	เข็มขัด
Too-ra-sàp	Telephone	โทรศัพท์
chút-chán-nai	Underpants	ชุดชั้นใน
chút-wâai náam	Swimsuit	ชุดว่ายน้ำ

Useful expression

What is this?	nîi à-rai?
How many baht is this one?	an-níi gìi Baht.
How much for that one?	an-nán tâo-rai.
Can you give me a discount?	lót dâi-mái?
Can I try it on?	lɔɔng dâi-mái?
I want this one	ao an-níi
Will you take it?	ao mái?
I won't take it	mâi ao
Change	ngən-tɔɔn
How old are you?	kun aa-yú tâo-rài?
How old are you?	kun aa-yú gìi bpii?
What is your phone number?	bəə too-rà-sàp kun àrai?

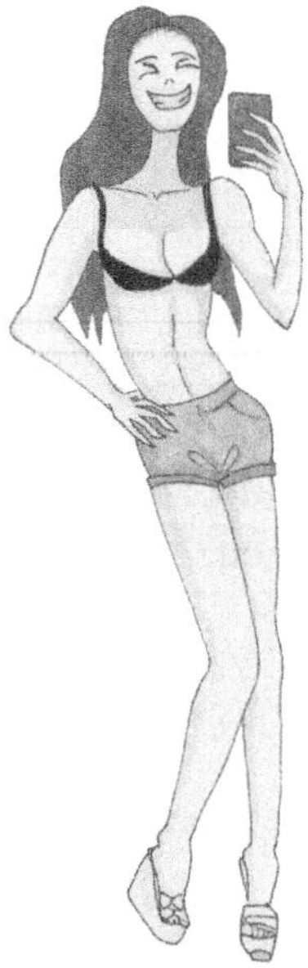

What is this? (nîi à-rai?)

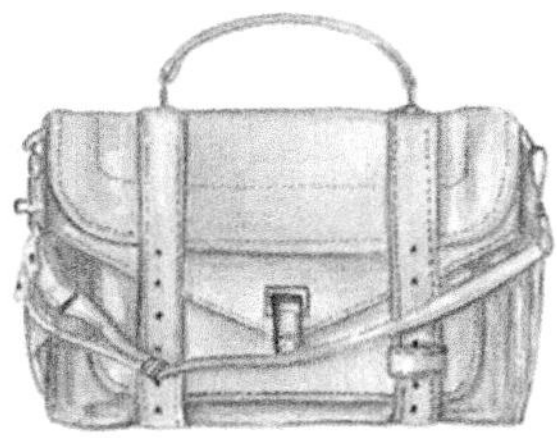

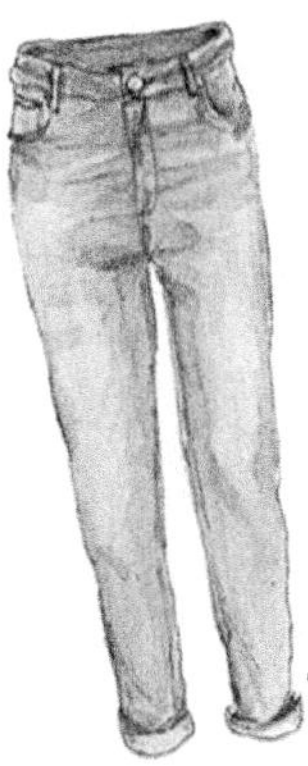

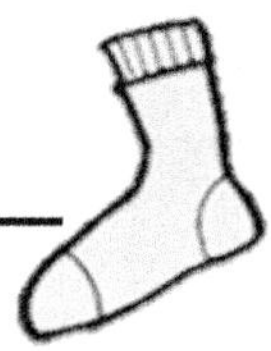

Exercise

1.Ang: sa wàt dii. sʉ̂a tâo-rài k.?

Tom: 199 baht k.

2.Ang: ________________	How much is this?
Tom: 1,000 baht k.	1,000 Baht.
Ang: lót dâi mái k.?	Can you give me a discount?
Tom: ______________	I can't.
Ang: ______________	That's alright.
3.Ang: dtua níi ___________ k?	How much is this shirt?
Tom: ___________________baht k.	500 Baht.
Ang: ___________________?	Can you give me a discount?
Tom: lót dâi 100 baht k. ao mái	I can. 100 Baht. will you take it?
Ang: ao kâ	OK
4. Tom: _____ raa-kaa gìi baht ?	How many Baht is that?
Ang: 200 baàt k.	200 Baht.
Tom: ____________________?	Can you give me a discount?
Ang: kɔ̌ɔ tôt. mâi dâi.	I'm sorry, I Can't.
Tom: ______________________k.	That's alright.

LESSON 4

Daily Activities ____________

Action verbs

bpai	bpai tîaw	maa	glàp
Go	Travel	Come	Return back
ไป	ไปเที่ยว	มา	กลับ

ráan aahǎan	a me ri gaa	rong rian	bâan
Restaurant	America	School	House
ร้านอาหาร	อเมริกา	โรงเรียน	บ้าน

PATTERN PRACTICE

chǎn	bpai	ráan aahǎan
pǒm	bpai tîaw	a me ri gaa
káo	maa	Rong rian
Tom	glàp	bâan

bpai which means **go** can be used for any situation where you are going to go somewhere. Shopping, Work, School etc.

bpai tîaw which means **travel** is used only when you are going somewhere for fun or enjoyment. Not for work or business. The location does not necessarily need to be far away. You could bpai tîaw to the local park.

Most Thai people use **pák pɔ̀ɔn** which means to **rest** or **relax** when going on holiday.

- bpai pák-pɔ̀ɔn tîi Phuket Go and relax at Phuket
- bpai pák-pɔ̀ɔn gàp faen Go and relax with boyfriend / girlfriend

Go to see/ Come to see

bpai hǎa	maa hǎa
Go to see	Come to see
ไปหา	มาหา

pʉ̂an	faen	pɔ̂ɔ	mâe
Friend	Boyfriend/Girlfriend	Father	Mother
เพื่อน	แฟน	พ่อ	แม่

PATTERN PRACTICE

chǎn	bpai hǎa	pʉ̂an
pǒm	bpai hǎa	faen
káo	maa hǎa	pɔ̂ɔ
Tom	maa hǎa	mâe

bpai yîam	maa yîam
Go to visit	Come to visit
ไปเยี่ยม	มาเยี่ยม

The word **yîam** (visit)
Only used when you are visiting people in the following situations:

- People in hospital (sick)
- People who live far away
- People who you have not met for a long time

chán bpai yîam pʉ̂an tîi Rong-pa-yaa-baan
pǒm bpai yîam krɔ̂ɔp-krua tîi Australia

gin	taan	dʉʉm
Eat	Eat (formal)	Drink
กิน	ทาน	ดื่ม

aa-hǎan	kâao	bia	náam
Food	Rice	Beer	Water
อาหาร	ข้าว	เบียร์	น้ำ

PATTERN PRACTICE

I eat/drink...

chǎn	gin	aa-hǎan	I eat food.
pǒm	taan	kâao	I eat food.
káo	dʉ̀ʉm	bia	He drinks beer.
rao	dʉ̀ʉm	náam	We drink water.

Gin

You can use gin for everything that you put in your stomach.

gin kâao	Eat rice
gin aa-hǎan	Eat food
gin Bia	Eat beer/drink beer
gin náam	Eat water/drink water
gin yaa	Eat medicine/take medicine or pill

gin kâao
When going out to eat, Thai people will always say **'bpai gin kâao'** even if they're going to eat pizza or noodles because gin kâao also means to "have a meal." Not necessarily to eat rice.

tam To make/To do ทำ

ngaan Job/Work งาน	aa-hǎan Food อาหาร	gaan-bâan Homework การบ้าน	sǔan Garden สวน

PATTERN PRACTICE

chǎn	chɔ̂ɔp	tam	ngaan	I like to work.
pǒm	chɔ̂ɔp	tam	aa-hǎan	I like to cook.
káo	mâi chɔ̂ɔp	tam	gaan- bâan	He doesn't like to do his homework.
rao	mâi chɔ̂ɔp	tam	sǔan	We don't like gardening.

lên Play เล่น

gii-laa Sport กีฬา	don-dtrii Music ดนตรี	bpia-noo Piano เปียโน	game Game เกมส์

Note: The word lên (play) is not always used the same way as it would be in English

You can use lên + verb to indicate that the verb is not being done seriously.

Example: nɔɔn lên, nâng lên, duu lên

sʉ́ʉ	kǎai	châao
Buy	Sell	Rent
ซื้อ	ขาย	เช่า

bâan	rót	con-doo	nǎng-sʉ̌ʉ
House	Car	Condominium	Book
บ้าน	รถ	คอนโด	หนังสือ

PATTERN PRACTICE

chán yàak sʉ́ʉ bâan	I want to buy a house.
káo kǎai aa-hǎan tîi dtà-làat	He/she sells food at the market.
pʉ̂an châao condo glâi Rong-rian	My friend rents a condo near school.
Ang sʉ́ʉ nǎng-sʉ̌ʉ	Ang bought a book.

duu	hěn
Look/ Watch	See
ดู	เห็น

Tv	nǎng	dèk	puu-kǎao/Doi
TV	Movie	Kids	Mountain
ทีวี	หนัง	เด็ก	ภูเขา/ดอย

PATTERN PRACTICE

mâe chɔ̂ɔp duu TV tîi bâan	Mum likes to watch TV at home.
pǒm hěn dèk lên computer	I saw a kid playing computer.
chán chɔ̂ɔp duu puu-kǎao/Dɔɔi	I like to look at the mountains.
chán hěn puu-kǎao/Dɔɔi	I saw the mountain.

rian
Study
เรียน

pûut	fang	àan	kǐan
Speak	Listen	Read	Write
พูด	ฟัง	อ่าน	เขียน

paa-sǎa
Language
ภาษา

Thai	Jiin	Ang grìt	Yîi bpùn
Thai	Chinese	English	Japan
ไทย	จีน	อังกฤษ	ญี่ปุ่น

PATTERN PRACTICE

chán yàak pûut paa-sǎa Thai	I want to speak Thai.
pǒm rian paa-sǎa Thai tîi Rong-rian	I study Thai at school.
kun Tom àan paa-sǎa Thai gèng	Mr. Tom can read Thai very well.
kun Robert kǐan paa-sǎa Jiin dâi nít-nɔ̀ɔi	Mr. Robert can write some Chinese.

dəən	wîng	wâai-náam	ɔ̀ɔk-gamlang-gaai	chók-muai
Walk	Run	Swim	Exercise	Boxing
เดิน	วิ่ง	ว่ายน้ำ	ออกกำลังกาย	ชกมวย

PATTERN PRACTICE

ta-mai fàràng chɔ̂ɔp dəən? Why do westerners like to walk?

rao bpai wîng We went jogging.

Eve mâi chɔ̂ɔp ɔ̀ɔk-gamlang-gaai Eve doesn't like to exercise.

fàràng chɔ̂ɔp rian chók-muai Westerners like to study boxing.

wâai-náam tîi bâan Swim at home.

nɔɔn làp	kui	pák-pɔ̀ɔn	rɔ́ɔng pləng	dtên
Sleep	Converse/Talk	Take a rest	Sing	Dance
นอนหลับ	คุย	พักผ่อน	ร้องเพลง	เต้น

PATTERN PRACTICE

dèk dtɔ̂ɔng nɔɔn-làp Kids need sleep.

chán kui gàp pʉ̂an fáràng I spoke with my caucasian friend.

kun Ang rɔ́ɔng-pləng gèng mâak Ms. Ang sing very well.

chán yàak dtên gàp kun I want to dance with you.

kun mâi sà-baai dtɔ̂ɔng pák-pɔ̀ɔn You're sick. You must take a rest.

Using verbs

Thai language does not use much time tense. Tenses are very simple and easy in Thai. Tense does not change form but we've added some words to emphasize and show time tense when you want to make it clear.

Present Continuous

For Present Continuous there are two words that can be used to emphasize actions.
The word **Gam-lang** is placed before the verb.
The word **yùu** is placed after the verb.
They can also be used together; **Gam-lang....... yùu**

gam-lang.....	.....yùu	gam-lang....... yùu
Emphasizes that the action is going on	Emphasizes that the state exists	Is in progress
กำลัง	อยู่	กำลัง...อยู่

What are you doing?

Kun tam àrai yùu?

I'm eating
chán gam-lang gin kâao
chán gin kâao yùu
chán gam-lang gin kâao yùu

I'm cooking
chán gam-lang tam aa-hǎan
chán tam aa-hǎan yùu
chán gam-lang tam aa-hǎan yùu

I'm studying
chán gam-lang rian
chán rian yùu
chán gam-lang rian yùu

Past tense

For past tense we add **láew,** which means **already,** after the verb.

láew	maa
Already	Have been
แล้ว	มา

PATTERN PRACTICE

gin kâao láew — Have eaten already.

glàp bâan láew — Went back home already.

Future tense

Add **jà,** which means **will,** before the verb.

jà
Will
จะ

PATTERN PRACTICE

What will you do?

kun jà tam àrai? — What will you do?

I will ....

chán jà bpai rong-rian — I will go to school.

chán jà tam aa-hǎan — I will cook.

pǒm jà rian paa-sǎa Thai — I will study Thai.

tîi-sùt

The most/the best

ที่สุด

PATTERN PRACTICE

What you like to do the most?

kun chɔ̂ɔp tam àrai tîi-sùt ?	What do you like to do the most?
pǒm chɔ̂ɔp wâai-náam tîi-sùt	I like to swim the most.
Jenny chɔ̂ɔp tam aa-hǎan tîi-sùt	Jenny likes to cook the most.
chán chɔ̂ɔp rian paa-sǎa Thai tîi-sùt	I like to study Thai the most.
káo chɔ̂ɔp bpai-tîaw Chiangmai tîi-sùt	I like travelling in chiangmai the most.

The word lên (play)

If a verb is followed by lên it usually means that action is not being done seriously.

dəən-lên	Go for a walk
pûut-lên	Joking
chʉ̂ʉ-lên	Nickname
kɔ̌ɔng-lên	Toy
nɔɔn-lên	Lay down and relax
nâng-lên	Sit down and relax

Maybe/Might

aàt-jà Maybe อาจจะ

PATTERN PRACTICE

chán àat-jà bpai rian paa-săa Thai tîi bprà-têet Thai (mʉang Thai)	I might study Thai in Thailand.
káo àat-jà mâi chɔ̂ɔp aa-hăan pèt	Maybe he doesn't like spicy food.
kun Peter àat-jà mâi maa	Mr. Peter might not come.
prûng-níi àat-jà chuan mâe bpai wâai-náam	I might invite mum to go swimming tomorrow.

Can/able to

dâi Can ได้	bpen Able to (skill) เป็น

The word "**dâi**"
"dâi" means can. It is used at the end of a statement when you want to indicate the ability or possibility.
"**dâi-măi**" is a question. It is a compound question word combining "**dâi**" which means can; able to; possible to' and "**măi**" which is a Yes/No question word. 'Can......?' 'Could......?'
In Thai we always put question words at the end of sentence.

PATTERN PRACTICE

chán bpai bâan kun dâi mái?	Can I go to your house?
fá-ràng sʉ́ʉ bâan tîi bprà-têet Thai dâi măi?	Can foreigners buy a house in Thailand?
kun pûut paa-săa Thai dâi mái?	Can you speak Thai?

Answer

dâi	I can.
mâi-dâi	I can't.

The word "**bpen**"
Means "can" and is used with a skill or something which is learnt. For example; Swimming, playing an instrument or riding a bike. "Is the subject able to do something?" (focus on skills.)
"**mâi-bpen**" means incapable due to not knowing how to do something. Or due to no experience

PATTERN PRACTICE

kun wâai-náam bpən mái?	Can you swim?
kun pûut paa-săa Thai bpən mái?	Can you speak Thai?
lên tennis bpən mái?	Can you play Tennis?
tam aa-hăan bpən mái?	Can you cook?

Ever/Never

kəəi	mâi kəəi
Ever/Have experience	Never/Never experienced
เคย	ไม่เคย

PATTERN PRACTICE

kun kəəi gin aa-hăan Jiin mái?	Have you ever eaten Chinese food?
chán kəəi bpai Phuket	I've been to Phuket.
Tom kəəi yùu Chiangmai	Tom has lived in Chiang Mai.
pŏm mâi kəəi jəə káo	I've never met him.

wǎi

Can (Physically capable)

ไหว

The word **wǎi** also means can and is used when you're not expected to be able to do something. It is related to physical capability and willpower.

.... + wǎi-mǎi

Examples:

Q: kun mâi sàbaai tam-ngaan wǎi mái?	You're sick, can you still work?
A1: wǎi	Yes, I can.
A2: mâi wǎi	No, I can not.

Q: kun dəən wǎi mái?	Can you walk?
A1: wǎi	Yes, I can.
A2: mâi wǎi	No, I can not.

Useful expression

What are you doing?	kun tam àrai yùu?
Do you want to eat together?	gin-kâao dûai-gan mái?
Could you please speak up?	pûut dang-dang nɔ̀ɔi.
(I) didn't hear.	mâi dâi yin.
Could you please speak slowly?	pûut cháa-cháa nɔ̀ɔi.
Again / Once more.	ìik tii.
Hurry up.	rîip rîip.
What is this called in Thai?	nîi paa-săa Thai rîak-wâa àrai?
(I) don't understand.	mâi kâo-jai.
(I) don't remember	jam mâi dâi.
I'm looking but I can't see (it)	mɔɔng mâi hĕn.

LESSON 5

Food and Drink

How Thai people eat:
Thai people like to eat together with many different kinds of foods in the centre of the floor or table so that everybody can easily access all of the food. They eat like this both at home with family or when going out to a restaurant. Thai restaurants will usually operate the same way; you each have an empty plate and all of the dishes are placed in the middle of the table so you can pick and choose what you wish to eat.
Thai people usually go kind of crazy with the condiments. A simple noodle bowl is not complete without adding another 10 kinds of sauce, chili, sugar and peanuts.
Thais use a spoon and a fork for almost every dish. Chopsticks are available most of the time and no matter how long you have been here you will still have the odd friend comment "wow you can use chopsticks!"
Use the spoon to bring food to your mouth and use the fork to push food on to the spoon.
Usually, one person will serve up food to everybody else at the table. If that person happens to be you then make sure to serve the older people first and yourself last.
When serving yourself you should use the serving spoon and not your own spoon for hygine reasons.
If you want to use a toothpick at the end of the meal then cover your mouth while you use it. You might have already noticed your Thai friends doing this.

Food

aa-hǎan Food อาหาร	gàp-kâao (with rice) Food/Main dish กับข้าว

Cooking styles & Methods

pàt Stir fry ผัด	tɔ̂ɔt Fry ทอด	gaeng Curry แกง

dtôm To boil ต้ม	bpîng/yâang To barbeque ปิ้ง/ย่าง	nʉ̂ng To steam นึ่ง	òb To bake อบ

Meats

gài Chicken ไก่	mǔu Pork หมู	bplaa Fish ปลา

gûng Shrimp/Prawn กุ้ง	nʉ́a Beef เนื้อ	bpèd Duck เป็ด

Some Thai people try to avoid eating beef because we believe that this animal assists agriculture. Better to say that Thai people don't eat a lot of beef. Additionally, there is not a lot of beef cattle raised in the country. Pork, chicken and fish are more commonly consumed by Thai people.

Never flip a fish

Maybe you have heard this said before?

This is an old fisherman superstition and is usually only observed in the ocean area; the South and the East of Thailand. They believe that once you turn the fish over (to access the flesh on the other side), a boat will be similarly capsized in the ocean.

Some people are very strict about this and will remove the bones instead from the middle of the fish in order to access the flesh on the other side. Personally, I have never seen a northern or anyone from Bangkok care.

Popular Thai dishes

dtôm-yam gûng	Spicy Shrimp Soup	ต้มยำกุ้ง
gaeng Kiaw wǎan gài	Green Chicken Curry	แกงเขียวหวานไก่
Pàt grà-prao	Meat or Seafood Fried with Sweet Basil	ผัดกระเพรา
Pàd Thai	Thai Style Fried Noodles	ผัดไทย
gaeng pèt bpèd yâang	Roast Duck Curry	แกงเผ็ดเป็ดย่าง
dtôm kàa gài	Chicken in Coconut Soup	ต้มข่าไก่
gài pàt mét má-muâng-hǐmmápaan	Chicken Fried with Cashew Nuts	ไก่ผัดเม็ดมะม่วงหิมพานต์
gaeng Pá naeng	Meat in Coconut Cream	แกงพะแนง
sôm-dtam	Papaya Salad	ส้มตำ
kâao-nǐaw mǔu bpîng	Sticky Rice with Grilled Pork	ข้าวเหนียวหมูปิ้ง

How to order food

kɔ̌ɔ..........nɔ̀ɔi
May I have..........please
ขอ...............หน่อย

ao.......... kâ/kráp
I want ....
เอา...............ค่ะ/ครับ

sàng..........
To order..........
สั่ง...............ค่ะ/ครับ

Can I have/Order....

kɔ̌ɔ............nɔ̀ɔi

ao............

sàng.........

jaan	chaam	tûay	tîi
Plate	Bowl	Cup	An order
จาน	ชาม	ถ้วย	ที่

PATTERN PRACTICE

kɔ̌ɔ kâao 2 jaan	Can I have 2 plates of rice.
kɔ̌ɔ dtôm-yam-gûng 1 chaam	Can I have 1 bowl of spicy shrimp soup.
ao kâao-pàt 2 tîi	I would like 2 more fried rice.

With/Without

sài	mâi sài
To put in	Not put in
ใส่	ไม่ใส่

prík	pǒng chuu rót	pàk
Chili	MSG	Vegetable
พริก	ผงชูรส	ผัก

náam-dtaan	glʉʉa	má-kʉ̌a-têet
Sugar	Salt	Tomato
น้ำตาล	เกลือ	มะเขือเทศ

PATTERN PRACTICE

ao an-níi mâi sài prík	I'll take this one, no chili.
mâi sài pǒng-chuu-rót	No MSG.
mâi sài náam-dtaan	No sugar.

Take away

sài tǔng	ao glàp bâan
Put in plastic bag (take away)	Take back home (take away)
ใส่ถุง	เอากลับบ้าน

gin tîi-nîi	taan tîi-nîi
Eat here	Eat here
กินที่นี่	ทานที่นี่

PATTERN PRACTICE

sài tǔng	Put in a plastic bag.
ao glàp bâan	Take away.

Bill please

dtang/ ngən Money ตังค์/เงิน	dtíp Tip ทิป

gəp dtang/gəp ngən Bill please เก็บตังค์/เก็บเงิน	chék bin Bill please เช็คบิล

PATTERN PRACTICE

gəp dtang/gəp ngən	Bill please.
chék bin	Bill please.
ngən tɔɔn	Change.
mâi dtɔ̂ɔng tɔɔn	No need to give me the change.
chán/pǒm líang	It's my treat.

Tipping in Thailand
Tipping seems to depend on Social-class. Sometimes people will leave a tip to keep face. That is to show that they are higher class.
At other times people simply tip because they are happy with the service.
Thais generally don't tip at street food restaurants. Though for the middle-class who eat at more expensive places and can afford to tip. They want to prove that "I have enough to eat here and i have enough to leave a tip"
Most people can afford to leave at least a 10-20 Baht tip while also understanding that people who earn 300 THB/day can't leave 20 or 30 THB. This amount could be their next meal.

Utensils

chɔ̂ɔn	sɔ̂ɔm	dtà-gìap
Spoon	Fork	Chopsticks
ช้อน	ส้อม	ตะเกียบ

mîit	tǔng	máai-jîm-fan
Knife	Plastic bag	Toothpick
มีด	ถุง	ไม้จิ้มฟัน

PATTERN PRACTICE

kon Thai cháai chɔ̂ɔn gàp sɔ̂ɔm	Thais use a spoon and fork.
chán cháai dtà-gìap mâi bpen	I can't use chopsticks.
mîit yùu nǎi?	Where is the knife?
mâi ao tǔng	I don't need a plastic bag.

Useful expressions

Can I have the menu please.	kɔ̌ɔ Menu nɔ̀ɔi kâ/kráp.
Can I have the English menu please.	kɔ̌ɔ Menu paa-sǎa Angrìt nɔ̀ɔi kâ/kráp.
I would like to order please.	kɔ̌ɔ sàng aa-hǎan nɔ̀ɔi kâ/kráp.
What do you have?	mii àrai bâang?
Do you have any to reccommend?	mii àrai náe-nam mái?
I will take this one.	ao an níi.
I would like to order more.	sàng aa-hǎan pə̂əm.
Do you want anything else?	ao àrai pə̂əm mái?
Want (something) more.	ao...... ìik
No need to give me the change.	mâi dtɔ̂ɔng tɔɔn.
Put in a plastic bag / take away.	sài tǔng ao glàp bâan.

Noodles

gǔay-dtǐaw Noodle ก๋วยเตี๋ยว

sên yài Big strip เส้นใหญ่	sên lék Small strip เส้นเล็ก	sên mìi Vermicelli เส้นหมี่

bà-mìi Egg noodles บะหมี่	wún-sên Glass noodles วุ้นเส้น	ka-nǒm-jiin Fresh Shan style noodles ขนมจีน

PATTERN PRACTICE

gǔay-dtǐaw hǎa ngâai	Noodles are easy to find.
Tom chɔ̂ɔp gin sên yài	Tom likes to eat big strip noodles.
kɔ̌ɔ sên lék mǔu 1 chaam	Can I have 1 bowl of small strip noodles with pork.
ka-nǒm-jiin pèt dtàe àrɔ̀ɔi	Fresh Shan style noodles are spicy but delicious.

náam Water (with soup) น้ำ	hâeng Dry (without soup) แห้ง

PATTERN PRACTICE

gǔay-dtǐaw náam	Noodles in soup.
kɔ̌ɔ gǔay-dtǐaw sên lék mǔu hâeng	Can I have small strip noodles with pork, without soup.

Flavor

pɵ̀t	wǎan	bprîaw
Spicy	Sweet	Sour
เผ็ด	หวาน	เปรี้ยว

kɵm	kǒm	jʉ̀ʉt	man
Salty	Bitter	Plain/Tasteless	Oily
เค็ม	ขม	จืด	มัน

PATTERN PRACTICE

aa-hǎan Thai pɵ̀t mâak	Thai food is very spicy.
kon Thai chɔ̂ɔp wǎan	Thais like sweet flavour.
pǒn-là-máai bprîaw	Sour fruit.
sà-mǔn-prai kǒm	Herbs are bitter.
kon Thai kít-wâa aa-hǎan fàràng jʉ̀ʉt	Thais think western food is tasteless.

Thais like strong flavored food. They usually like it quite spicy too. Don't be afraid, just use these phrases if you don't enjoy a mouthful of fire.
mâi pèt - not spicy
pèt nít-nɔ̀ɔi - a litle bit spicy

Keep in mind if you order not spicy it will still be a bit spicy because chili and pepper are part of the recipe, they will just use less.

mâi sài prík - Without chili
mâi pèt ləəi - Not spicy at all

kâao Rice ข้าว

kâao bplào Plain rice ข้าวเปล่า	kâao sǔai Beautiful rice ข้าวสวย	kâao jâao Rice ข้าวจ้าว
Steamed rice		

kâao nǐaw Sticky rice ข้าวเหนียว	kâao glɔ̂ɔng Brown rice ข้าวกล้อง	kâao sǎan Uncooked rice ข้าวสาร

PATTERN PRACTICE

gin kâao nǐaw lá-gɔ̂ɔ ngûang-nɔɔn	Eat sticky rice and then feel sleepy.
kâao glɔ̂ɔng mii bprà-yòot	Brown rice is healthy.
kɔ̌ɔ kâao 1 tǒo	1 bowl of rice, please.

kâao râat gaeng ข้าวราดแกง
A plate of rice with many different kinds of topping to choose from. You will see this a lot in Thailand around food courts and street food carts. There are many kinds of food in seperate trays. You select 1-3 different toppings and it is served on top of rice. If you want more food you can pay an extra 5-10 Baht to get more.
This kind of dish is for one person. You don't need to share your food.

kài Egg ไข่

kài gài Chicken eggs ไข่ไก่	kài bpèd Duck eggs ไข่เป็ด	kài nók Quail eggs ไข่นก

PATTERN PRACTICE

kài nók lék mâak	Quail eggs are very small.
kài raa-kaa mâi paeng	Eggs are not expensive.
Kun dtɔ̂ɔng sʉ́ʉ kài gài sòt	You must buy fresh eggs.
kài bpèd àrɔ̀ɔi gwàa kài gàl	Duck eggs are more delicious than Chicken eggs.

Eggs menu

kài daao	Fried egg.
kài jiaw	Omelette.
kài dtôm	Boiled egg.
kài kon	Scrambled eggs.
kài lûak	Soft-boiled egg.
kài kem	Salted, preserved eggs.
kài yîaw máa	100-year-old eggs/ Pink eggs.
kài lûuk kěəi	Fried eggs with sweet sauce.

Vegetarian food

Being a vegan in Thailand is deeply tied to Buddhism. Buddists choose to be vegan because they believe in karma. They believe that when you save the life of another living creature you will in turn have a long life.
For some countries, there is no widely understood translation of the word "vegan", in Thailand this is not a problem. The concept of veganism or "**jee**" has been around for hundreds of years and is connected with Buddhist spiritual practices.

Being a vegan in Thailand is easy because traditional Thai cuisine is mostly composed of vegetables. You will find fruit stands at every corner and also fresh markets that are full of organic produce.
Look for this symbol:

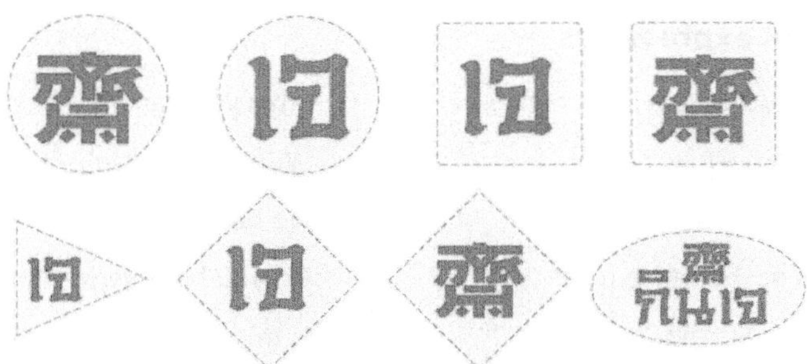

If you going to a normal restaurant without this symbol, you need to inform the staff that you are a Vegetarian.
It is also a good idea to specify that you don’t eat fish sauce because most restaurants tend to use it.

Vegetarian food

aa-hǎan jəə Vegetarian food อาหารเจ	gin jəə Eat vegetarian (food) กินเจ	mang-sà-wí-rát Vegetarian (formal term) มังสวิรัติ

Vegetarian menu

Put the word **jee** behind the name of food.

gaeng hèt jee	Vegetarian mushroom curry.
pàt pàk jee	Vegetarian fried vegetables.
gaeng jʉ̀ʉt jee	Vegetarian clear soup.
gaeng pèt jee	Vegetarian red curry.
dtôm yam jee	Vegetarian spicy soup.
pàt Thai jee	Vegetarian fried noodles, Thai style.

Useful expressions

chǎn/pǒm gin jəə	I'm a vegetarian.
sài dtâo-hûu	With tofu please.
mâi sài nʉ́a ləəi	No beef at all.
mii aa-hǎan jee mái?	Do you have vegetarian food?
an níi jee mái?	Is this vegetarian food?

Eat vegetarian food

The Thai Vegetarian Festival occurs annually in October.

The Thai Vegetarian Festival takes place for nine days. Some Thai people will choose to live by the Five Buddhist Precepts for a total of 10 days. Some of the events begin a day or two before, and can continue a day after, depending on the temple and organizing committee involved.

Weird foods

Most weird foods in Thailand are local foods **aa-hǎan pʉ́ʉn-mʉang.** Most parts of Thailand have their own unique (and weird) dishes.

bplaa-ráa	Pickled Fish
mà-laeng tɔ̂ɔt	Fried Insects
kài-mót-daeng	Egg Ants
gûng-dtên	Dancing Shrimp
nǔu-naa yâang	Rat of Heaven
lâap-lʉ̂at	Raw Beef in Uncooked Blood
kài kâao	Balut (bird embryo)

písèt means "Special" but for food it means a large serving or extra food.
tam-má-daa means normal or a normal serving size.
You can always request a "special" size in any Thai restaurant and pay around 5-20 baht more depend on the kind of food you are ordering.

Free drinks and free vetgetables
Most Thai restaurants will have self serve water and vegetables. Keep an eye out for it as bottled water costs 10-20 THB.

Western food

kà-nǒm bpang	Bread	ขนมปัง
kà-nǒm bpang bpîng	Toast	ขนมปังปิ้ง
saen-wít	Sandwich	แซนวิช
ham-bəə-gə̂ə	Burger	แฮมเบอเกอร์
man-fárang	Potato	มันฝรั่ง
man-fáràng tɔ̂ɔt	Chips	มันฝรั่งทอด
yaem	Jam	แยม
nəəi	Butter	เนย
haem	Ham	แฮม
sà-dték	Steak	สเต๊ก
sà-bpaa-gət-dtîi	Spaghetti	สปาเกตตี้

kà-nǒm bpang **bread**
Thais don't eat bread as a meal. They consider bread to be a snack or junk food and that only rice can be the "real" main course.
Over recent years as western influence increases this is changing and thai people are eating more bread because it is easy and convinient.

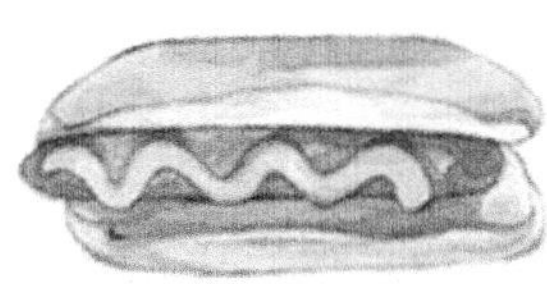

Drinks

In Thailand, most standard restaurants will provide free drinks but the higher end or luxury restaurants will charge you for bottled water.

náam	chaa	gaa-fae	nom
Water	Tea	Coffee	Milk
น้ำ	ชา	กาแฟ	นม

rɔ́ɔn	Yen
Hot	Cold/Ice
ร้อน	เย็น

PATTERN PRACTICE

kɔ̌ɔ náam yen — Can I have cold water?

chán mâi dʉ̀ʉm náam yen — I don't drink cold drinks.

kun yàak dʉ̀ʉm gaa-fae rɔ́ɔn mái? — Do you want to drink hot coffee?

ao chaa yen mâi sài nom 2 gâew kâ — I'll have 2 glasses of iced tea, no milk.

chaa yen mâi sài náam-dtaan kráp — Iced tea, no sugar.

bia	lâao	waai	náam pǒnlámái
Beer	Whisky	Wine	Fruit juice
เบียร์	เหล้า	ไวน์	น้ำผลไม้

gâew	kùat	náam kǎeng
Glass	Bottle	Ice
แก้ว	ขวด	น้ำแข็ง

PATTERN PRACTICE

Fàràng dʉʉm bia mâi sài náam-kǎeng	Westerners drink beer without ice.
bpà-gà-dtì káo gin bia 3 kùat	He usually drinks 3 bottles of beer.

lék	yài
Small	Big
เล็ก	ใหญ่

PATTERN PRACTICE

kɔ̌ɔ bia Sǐng kùat lék 1 kuàt	Can I have 1 small Singha beer?
kɔ̌ɔ bia Sǐng kùat yài1 kuàt	Can I have 1 big Singha beer?
cháng lék 1	1 small Chang beer.
bia Leo yài 1	1 big Leo beer.

Wait

rɔɔ To wait รอ

rɔɔ sák-krûu Wait for a moment (formal) รอสักครู่	rɔɔ bpáep-nʉ̀ng Wait for a second รอแป๊ปนึง

Useful vocabulary

Drunk	mao
Already	láew
All Gone	mòt
Pay	jàai
Don't	yàa
Enough	pɔɔ
Close	bpìt
Open	bpə̀ət

gin kâao dûai-gan mái?
Which means "Would you like to eat together?." You are going to hear this a lot from Thai people. It is common for a Thai person to invite you to eat with them. Sometimes they are only trying to be polite and expect you to refuse the offer but if they ask a second or third time it means they really want you to accept the invitation. The same is true of the reverse; If you ask a Thai person to eat with you, they will decline the first offer, but accept the second or third time.

LESSON 6

Fruits

The Kingdom of a Hundred Fruits

This is one of the reasons why people want to visit Thailand. Thailand's position as a tropical country means that we produce many different kinds of fruits and vegetables of good quality. Fruits in this country are so plentiful, so diversified, so inexpensive and so delicious.

Here is a brief introduction to several kinds of fruits produced in Thailand that are worth special recommendation. Names in Thai with their romanized spellings are given after the English names to facilitate the identification of the fruits. Prices given are just rough indicators. The actual prices may vary according to the season, the harvest and where the fruits are bought.

Fruits

pŏn-lá-máai	Fruit	ผลไม้
săow-wá-rót	Passionfruit	เสาวรส
sàp-pà-rót	Pineapple	สัปปะรด
má-mûang	Mango	มะม่วง
má-lá-gɔɔ	Papaya	มะละกอ
glûay	Banana	กล้วย
má-práao	Coconut	มะพร้าว
tú-rian	Durian	ทุเรียน
fàràng	Guava	ฝรั่ง
sôm	Orange	ส้ม
sôm-oo	Pomelo	ส้มโอ
mang-kút	Mangosteen	มังคุด
lam-yai	Longan	ลำไย
nɔ́ɔi-nàa	Sugar Apple	น้อยหน่า
dtaeng-mo	Watermelon	แตงโม
sà-dtɔɔ-bee-rîi	Strawberry	สตรอเบอรี่
ngɔ́	Rambutan	เงาะ
chom-pûu	Rose Apple	ชมพู่
chəə-rîi	Cherry	เชอร์รี่
à-ngùn	Grape	องุ่น
lín-jìi	Lychee	ลิ้นจี่
gâew-mang-gɔɔn	Dragon fruit	แก้วมังกร
kà-nŭn	Jack fruit	ขนุน
táp-tim	Pomegranate	ทับทิม
má-gɔ̀ɔk	Olive	มะกอก

sùk Ripe สุก	dìp Raw/Unripe ดิบ

PATTERN PRACTICE

an níi sùk mái?	Is this one ripe?
chán chɔ̂ɔp má-mûang dìp	I like unripe mango.
má-mûang sùk wǎan mâak	Ripe mango is so sweet.
kon jiin chɔ̂ɔp pǒn-lá-máai sùk	Chinese people like ripe fruits.
pǒn-lá-máai sùk àrɔ̀ɔi tîi-sùt	Ripe fruit is the most delicious.

sòt Fresh สด	hâeng Dry แห้ง	nâo/sǐa Rotten เน่า เสีย

PATTERN PRACTICE

pǒn-lá-máai sòt paeng	Fresh fruits are expensive.
Kon jiin chɔ̂ɔp sʉ́ʉ pǒn-lá-máai hâeng	Chinese like to buy dried fruits.
pǒn-lá-máai níi nâo láew	This fruit went bad.
pǒn-la-máai sòt dii gwàa pǒn-lá-máai hâeng	Fresh fruits are better than dried fruits.
tîi dtà-làat mii pǒn-lá-máai sòt yə́	At the market there are a lot fresh fruits.

lá Per ละ

giloo/loo Kilogram กิโลกรัม	lûuk/bai/pǒn Whole Fruit ลูก ใบ ผล	kìit 100 grams ขีด

tǔng Plastic Bag ถุง	chín Piece ชิ้น	krʉ̂ng Half ครึ่ง

PATTERN PRACTICE

giloo lá tâo-rai? — How much per kilogram?

tǔng lá tâo-rai? — How much per bag?

lûuk lá tâo-rai? — How much per item?

chín lá tâo-rai? — How much per piece?

giloo lá .... — ....per kigogram.

tǔng lá .... — ....per bag.

lûuk lá .... — ....per one.

chín lá .... — ....per piece.

How do you sell these fruits? (per box? per kilo? Etc)

There are many ways to sell fruit in Thailand and how they are sold depends on what type, what container or package and where they are being sold.

kǎai yang-ngai?	kǎai bpen..........
How do you sell (this)?	Sell per...
ขายยังไง	ขายเป็น

PATTERN PRACTICE

How much/many do you want?

ao gìi giloo?	How many kilos do you want?
ao gìi chín?	How many pieces do you want?

I would like to take

ao sôm 2 loo krʉ̂ng	I'll take 2 and a half kilos of oranges.
má mûang 2 lûuk	2 mangoes.

Seasonal Fruits

Summer	Mango, Jackfruit, Rambutan, Watermelon, Lychee, Rose Apple, Mangosteen, Papaya, Banana
Rainy season	Banana, Pomelo, Longan, Guava, Star fruit, Grape, Custard Apple, Durian
Cold season	Sugar Cane, Grape, Strawberry, Rose Apple, Tamarind
All season	Grape, Orange, Banana, Guava, Apple, Pineapple, Rose Apple

Durian
The King of fruit

"Tastes Like Heaven, Smells Like Hell" This can accurately describe Durian.
Durian is an aggressive looking fruit with a lot of thorns covering the exterior. It's native and common throughout all parts of Southeast Asia. In Thailand, Malaysia, Indonesia and the Philippines Durian is well known for its incredibly strong smell. Sometimes compared to sewage, rotting flesh or, at best, ripe cheese. If compare to other fruits Durian is the most expensive.

In Thailand, hotels and airlines do not allow you to bring durian inside. It is also illegal to bring it on to any public transportation because of the smell.

In Malaysia, it is illegal to eat durian in public.

Durian is a strange combination of mildly sweet, creamy and savoury with a whiff of alcohol.
Thais believe Durian will cause "internal heat" inside your body when you eat too much and that you should not consume durian with alcohol.

Mangosteen
The Queen of fruit

Mangosteen is the national fruit of Thailand. It grows throughout all of Southeast Asia and originated in Indonesia.

Mangosteen is a small, round purple fruit with a golden sepal on top which looks like a crown. She is the queen and her shell is bulky and purple while her heart is tender and sweet. Mangosteen is sweet and tangy with a juicy and somewhat fibrous texture. Like a combination of strawberry and peach. Its purplish pigment has also been used as a dye.

During harvest season and especially in July you can find mountains of mangosteen at every street corner for 15 to 30 baht per kilo (between fifty cents and one dollar). Buy plenty while they are in season and then move on to the next seasonal fruit. Thailand is never lacking delicious, cheap fruit.

Slang words from Fruits

guâi means Banana

guâi-guâi is means easy or "piece of cake" in English.

sà-dtɔɔ-bəə-rîi strawberry
Actually, this word is word is quite new. sà-dtɔɔ-bəə-rîl is the polite version of the word and dtɔɔ-lǎe is the "street" version which means Bulls..t / Bull crap

Conversation

Sam: sa wàt dii kráp.

Seller: sa wàt dii jáa.

Sam: mii pǒn-lá-máai arai bâang?

Seller: mii má-mûang, sǎow-wà-rót, dtaeng-mo láe à-ngùn

Sam: má-mûang kǎai yang-ngai?

Seller: kǎai bpen giloo kâ.

Sam: giloo lá tâo-rài K?

Seller: giloo lá 60 Bath K

Sam: bprîaw mái K?

Seller: mâi bprîaw K wǎan mâak K.

ao gìi giloo K?

Sam: 1 giloo krʉ̂ng tâo-rài?

Seller: 1 giloo krʉ̂ng 90 Bath K

Sam: ao 2 giloo K. lót dâi-mái?

Seller: lót 20 bath k.

Sam: kɔ̀ɔp kun k.

tîi-sùt

The most

ที่สุด

PATTERN PRACTICE

kun chɔ̂ɔp pŏn-lá-máai àrai tîi-sùt?	Which fruit do you like the most?
tú-rian paeng tîi-sùt.	Durian is the most expensive.
má-muâng dìp bprîaw tîi-sùt.	Raw mango is the sourest.
pŏn-lá-mái ruam	Mixed fruits.

ìik

More/Another

อีก

PATTERN PRACTICE

ao àrai ìik mái?	Would you like anything else?
ao kâao ìik 2 jaan	I'll have two more rice.
ao ìik	I want more.
kɔ̌ɔ Beer ìik	Can I have more beer?
pûut ìik	Say again?

gəən bpai

Too much

เกินไป

PATTERN PRACTICE

aa-hăan Thai pèt gəən-bpai	Thai food is too spicy.
gaa-fae gâew níi rɔ́ɔn gəən-bpai	This cup of coffee is too hot.
kà-nŏm Thai wăan gəən-bpai	Thai desserts are too sweet.

mâi kɔ̂ɔi

Not really/ Not so

ไม่ค่อย

PATTERN PRACTICE

wan-níi mâi kɔ̂ɔi rɔ́ɔn	Today is not so hot.
chán mâi kɔ̂ɔi hǐw	I'm not so hungry.
aa-hǎan tîi ráan níi mâi kɔ̂ɔi àrɔ̀ɔi	This shop foods are not so delicious.

Useful vocab

A lot	yə́
To take	ao
Like	chɔ̂ɔp
Also/As well	dûai
Give	hâi
Called that	rîak-wâa
Say that	pûut-wâa
Tell that	bɔ̀ɔk-wâa
Think that	kít-wâa
Means...	bpae-wâa

Polite Requests

In Thai we classify requests into two categories according to the speaker's purpose as follows:

chûai which means help
When you want to ask a person to do you a favour.

chûai pûut cháa cháa nɔ̀ɔi kŕap	Could you please speak slowly?
chûai bpə̀ət bprà-dtuu nɔ̀ɔi dâi-mái?	Can you help open the door please?
chûai sʉ́ʉ náam hâi chán nɔ̀ɔi dâi-mái?	Could you please buy me a water?

kɔ̌ɔ which means May I?
When you want to ask for something.

kɔ̌ɔ duu nɔ̀ɔi	May I have a look?
kɔ̌ɔ sôm nɔ̀ɔi kráp	May I have an orange?
khɔ̌ɔ naám nɔ̀ɔi	May I have some water?
kɔ̌ɔ pûut gàp kun John nɔ̀ɔi kráp	May I speak with John?

*for "kɔ̌ɔ" and "chûai" request you can also add "dâai mái" which means "is it possible?" at the end of the sentence.

LESSON 7

Time

Have you heard that thai people are always late? (Thai time)

This relates to Thai culture. It is important for us to to be nice to one another and to forgive and sympathize. Thai culture is flexible that's why time is also flexible.

In the countryside things are more relaxed and people are very free flowing without caring to much for time. in Bangkok however everything is more or less on time.
It really depends on the situation. Thai people will get to work on time but social aren't as serious. If there is a benefit for them they will definitely turn up on time or just a little bit late.

This could be the reason words like **jai yen yen, sà-baai sà-baai (take it easy /relax/slowly/calm down)** exist in Thai.

mʉ̂a-rài?
When?
เมื่อไร

wan-níi	mʉ̂a-waan-níi	prûng-níi
Today	Yesterday	Tomorrow
วันนี้	เมื่อวานนี้	พรุ่งนี้

PATTERN PRACTICE

mʉ̂a-waan-níi kun tam àrai?	What did you do yesterday?
wan-níi chán yùu tîi bâan	Today I stayed at home.
kun bpai America mʉ̂a-rài?	When will you go to America?
wan-níi mâi yàak bpai tam-ngaan	I don't want to go to work today.

wan Day
aa-tít/sàp-daa Week
dʉan Month
bpii Year

......tîi-láew Last
......níi This
......nâa Next

PATTERN PRACTICE

wan-níi	Today
wan-tîi-l<u>áe</u>w	The day before
wan-nâa	Future/Following day
aa-tít-níi	This week
aa-tít-tîi-l<u>áe</u>w	Last week
aa-tít-nâa	Next week
dʉan-níi	This month
dʉan-tîi-l<u>áe</u>w	Last month
dʉan-nâa	Next month
bpii-níi	This year
bpii-tîi-l<u>áe</u>w	Last year
bpii-nâa	Next year

Day of the week

wan-jan	Monday	วันจันทร์
wan-ang-kaan	Tuesday	วันอังคาร
wan-pút	Wednesday	วันพุธ
wan-pá-rʉ́-hàt (sà bɔɔ dii)	Thursday	วันพฤหัสบดี
wan-sùk	Friday	วันศุกร์
wan-sǎao	Saturday	วันเสาร์
wan-aa-tít	Sunday	วันอาทิตย์

wan-nǎi?

Which day?

วันไหน

PATTERN PRACTICE

rao jà jəə-gan wan-nǎi?	Which day will we meet each other?
kun mii bprà-chum wan-nǎi?	Which day do you have a meeting?
wii-sâa kun mòt-aayú wan-nǎi?	Which day does your visa expire?
kun yàak bpai duu nǎng wan-nǎi?	Which day do you want to watch a movie?

wan-sǎao-aa-tít Weekend วันเสาร์อาทิตย์	wan-tam-má-daa Weekday วันธรรมดา

wan-yùt Holiday/Day off วันหยุด	wan-prá Buddha day วันพระ	wan-tîi Date (number) วันที่

PATTERN PRACTICE

sǎao-aa-tít níi rao jà bpai Lao — We're going to Laos this weekend.

wan-tam-má-daa káo tam-ngaan — He works on weekdays.

wan-yùt bpài tîaw dii mái? — Let's go to travel on our day off.

wan-gə̀ət kun wan-tîl àrai? — What date is your birthday?

wan-prá kon Thai bpai wát — Thais go to the temple on Buddha day.

gə̀ət To be born เกิด

PATTERN PRACTICE

kun gə̀ət mʉ̂a-rai? — When were you born?

wan-gə̀ət kun — Your birthday.

chán gə̀ət... — I was born...

What Day of the Week Were You Born?

What day of the week were you Born?

All Thais know what day of the week they were born.

One of the interesting aspects of Thai Buddhism is that there is a special Buddha pose for each of the seven days of the week.

In some temples you will see eight statues of Buddha aligned next to each other, often with a donation cup in front of it. People will pay respect to the statue representing the day they were born.

Don't be surprised when your friends ask you what *day* you were born. You might think they misspoke and that they actually want your *date* of birth. In ancient times the seven days of the week were named after the planets in our solar system. People believe that these planets can influence your character and behavior. Many Thais believe that their day of birth reflects their life.

The meaning of birthdays

SUNDAY | THE SUN

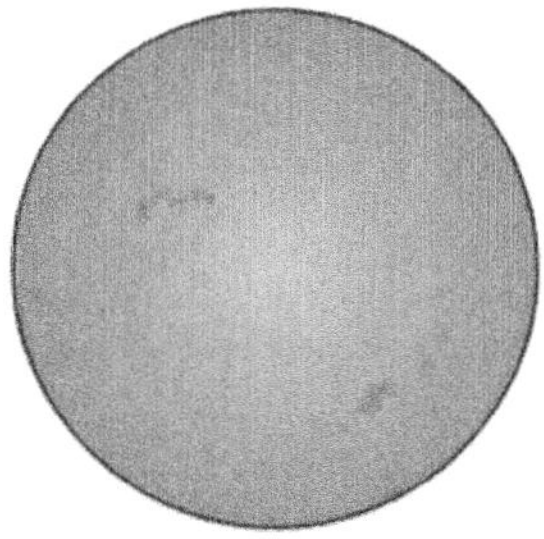

People born on this day, will never be satisfied with anything ordinary
in their lives and they will always be like a ray of sunshine for those around them with their bright auras. A child of Sunday is creative, noble, proud, self-centered, bold and loud. A person born on a Sunday is respectable, wise, loved by friends and family. They are likely to be in a professional occupation.

MONDAY |THE MOON

The Moon is changeable and plays a big role in their lives. Monday is the second day of the week. So a child born on this day will derive great satisfaction with whatever they have. Monday's child is kind, modest, motherly, adaptable, sensitive and possessive. A person born on a Monday is serious with a good memory and a love of travel. This person is likely to be in a skilled occupation.

TUESDAY | MARS

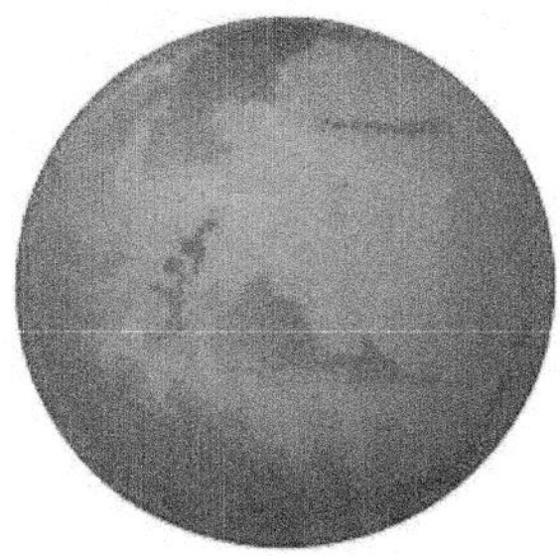

A person born on this day has the ruling planet of Mars, which symbolizes a fighting spirit, a desire to lead the way and a will to win. Tuesday's child is active, enthusiastic, energetic, courageous, brave, impatient though sometimes too fiery and destructive. They have a strong desire to achieve success. This person is serious, brave and active most probably in the services.

WEDNESDAY | MERCURY

Wednesday's child is communicative, logical, unreliable, careless and versatile. A person born on Wednesday morning is polite, artistic and emotional. They are most likely working creatively. Wednesday night is their lucky time and their lucky color is green.

THURSDAY | JUPITER

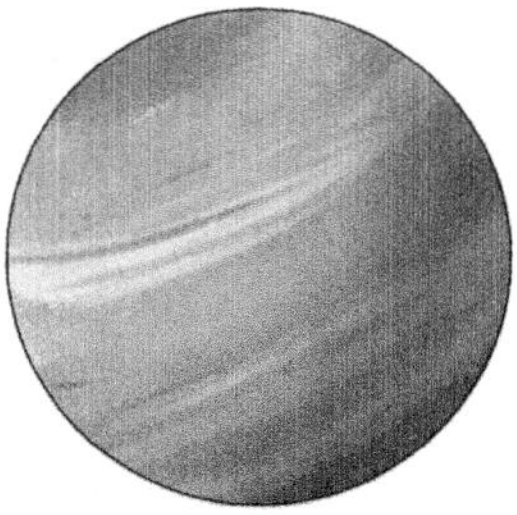

Jupiter symbolizes expansion, happiness, optimism, good humor and perspective, which means that Thursday's child will be jovial, generous, but also have the tendency for self-deception. This is a planet of teaching and a child born on a Thursday will always have a special philosophy to share with the world. This person is peaceful, calm and honest –likely to be a teacher or in the legal profession. Their lucky day is Sunday and their lucky color is orange.

FRIDAY | VENUS

Friday's child is under the rule of Venus, which is the planet of love, balance, beauty, affection, sharing, pleasure, colour, elegance, romance, artistry and refinement. Friday's child is social, seductive, artistic, lazy and sometimes too dependent on opinions of other people. This child needs to be surrounded by beauty and love, or their talents might remain hidden from the world and their joy subdued. This person is fun loving, friendly and ambitious, probably an entertainer or public figure. Their lucky day is Tuesday and their lucky color is pink.

SATURDAY | SATURN

Saturn's child has a strong resolve, is modest, slow and studious, tuned to other worlds and lifetimes. Saturday's child will be wise, professional, practical, strict and suspicious.
This person is calm, logical and a bit of a recluse. They are very likely engaged in manual work of a skilled nature. Their lucky day is Friday and their lucky color is blue.

Colours of the days in Thailand

The specific colour of each day depends on an astrological rule (influenced by Hindu mythology) that assigns a colour to each day of the week based on the colour of the God (or Navagraha) who protects that day.

Colours in Thailand matter. At least for part of the Buddhist population. In Thai tradition, there are colours that are considered lucky or unlucky for specific days of the week.
Colours mean so much that each day of the week is assigned a specific colour and in Thailand none of these colours are more important than yellow. This is because King Bhumibol was born on a Monday. Thai people decorate with yellow on their birthdays. Thai people often wear clothes corresponding to the colour of the day.

Day	Color of the day	Unlucky color	Celestial Body	God of the day
Sunday	Red	Blue	Sun	Surya
Monday	Yellow	Red	Moon	Chandra
Tuesday	Pink	Yellow; White	Mars	Mangala
Wednesday	Green	Pink	Mercury	Budha
Thursday	Orange	Purple	Jupiter	Brihaspati
Friday	Blue	Dark blue	Venus	Shukra
Saturday	Purple	Green	Saturn	Shani

gìi
How many
กี่

wan	aa-tít/sàp-daa	dʉan	bpii
Day	Week	Month	Year
วัน	อาทิตย์/สัปดาห์	เดือน	ปี

PATTERN PRACTICE

kun jà yùu tîi Yîi-bpùn gìi wan?	How many days will you be in Japan?
kun yùu mʉang Thai maa gìi bpii?	How many years have you been in Thailand?
kun rian paa-sǎa Thai gìi dʉan?	How many months have you studied Thai?
chán jà bpai pák-rɔ́ɔn tîi yú-rôop 2 aa-tít.	I'm going to vacation in Europe for 2 weeks

naan
Long time
นาน

PATTERN PRACTICE

naan mái?	It's take along time?
naan tâo-rài?	How long?
kun jà yùu Australia naan tâo-rài?	How long will you stay in Australia?
kun yùu tîi-nîi naan tâo-rài?	How long will you be here?
kun rian Thai naan tâo-rài?	How long have you been studying Thai?

Month

mók ga raa (kom)	January	มกราคม
gum paa (pan)	Febuary	กุมภาพันธ์
mii naa (kom)	March	มีนาคม
meh săa (yon)	April	เมษายน
prʉ́t sà paa (kom)	May	พฤษภาคม
mí tù naa (yon)	June	มิถุนายน
gà rá gà daa (kom)	July	กรกฎาคม
sĭng hăa (kom)	August	สิงหาคม
gan yaa (yon)	September	กันยายน
dtù laa (kom)	October	ตุลาคม
prʉ́t sà ji gaa (yon)	November	พฤศจิกายน
tan waa (kom)	December	ธันวาคม

NOTE: Adding kom/yon to the end depends on how many days are in the month. Kom means that month has 31 days, Yon means 30 days.

Period of Time

dtɔɔn At/In (time only) ตอน

cháao Morning เช้า	bàai Afternoon บ่าย	yen Evening เย็น

PATTERN PRACTICE

dtɔɔn cháao chán chɔ̂ɔp ɔ̀ɔk-gam-lang-gaai	I like to exercise in the morning.
dtɔɔn bàai rɔ́ɔn mâak	The afternoon is so hot.
dtɔɔn yen rót-dtìt mâak	In the evenings there are traffic jams.

glaang wan กลางวัน Day time	glaang kʉʉn กลางคืน Night time

PATTERN PRACTICE

pǒm chɔ̂ɔp glaang kʉʉn mâak gwàa (glaang wan)	I like night time more than day time.
dtɔɔn glaang wan rao bpai rong-rian	In the daytime we go to school.
dtɔɔn glaang kʉʉn rao pák-pɔ̀ɔn	In the night time we take a rest.

The word **mʉ̂a** will mean **last** if you put in front of a period of time.

cháao níi	This morning
kʉʉn níi	Tonight (this night)
mʉ̂a kʉʉn níi	Last night
mʉ̂a-waan-níi	Yesterday

dtɔɔn nǎi?
When
ตอนไหน

dtɔɔn níi	dtɔɔn nán	dtɔɔn tîi
Now	That time	When was
ตอนนี้	**ตอนนั้น**	**ตอนที่**

PATTERN PRACTICE

kun jà bpai-hǎa pʉ̂an dtɔɔn-nǎi?	When are you going to see your friend?
dtɔɔn-níi chǎn yùu tîi bâan faen	I'm at my boyfriend's house right now.
dtɔɔn-nán pǒm mâi chɔ̂ɔp káo	At that time I didn't like him.
dtɔɔn-tîi pǒm yùu tîi Angrìt,	When I was in England, I
pǒm pûut Thai mâi dâi.	couldn't speak Thai.

dǐaw níi **เดี๋ยวนี้** Right now/These days	mʉ̂a gîi níi **เมื่อกี้นี้** Just now

PATTERN PRACTICE

bpai àap-náam dǐaw-níi	Go to take a shower right now.
dǐaw-níi káo mâi kɔ̂ɔi sà-baai	He's sick right now.
mʉ̂a-gîi-níi pǒm jəə pʉ̂an gào	I just met an old friend.
mʉ̂a-gîi-níi pǒm pə̂əng gin kâao	I have just eaten food.

túk Every ทุก

wan Day วัน	Bpii Year ปี	kráng Time ครั้ง	yàng Kind อย่าง	Kon Person คน

PATTERN PRACTICE

túk-wan chán bpai wâai-náam gàp pʉ̂an	Everyday I go swimming with a friend.
túk-bpii rao bpai America	We go to America every year.
pǒm gin aa-hǎan túk-yàng	I eat every kind of food.
túk-kon chɔ̂ɔp rian paa-sǎa Thai	Everyone likes to study Thai.
túk-kráng lǎng-jàak wâai-náam, mâi sà-baal	He gets sick after swimming every káo time.

bɔ̀ɔi bɔ̀ɔi Often บ่อยๆ	sà-mə̌ə Always เสมอ

bpàk-gà-dtì Usually ปกติ	naan-naan-kráng Seldom/Everyone in a while นานๆครั้ง

PATTERN PRACTICE

mʉ̂a-waan-níi dtɔɔn-yen kun yùu tîi-nǎi?	Where were you yesterday evening?
dtɔɔn-bàai níi chán wâang, kun wâang mái?	This afternoon I'm free, are you free?
káo bpai lên gii-laa bɔ̀ɔi bɔ̀ɔi	I play sport often.
bpàk-gà-dtì chán mâi àab-náam dtɔɔn-cháao	Usually I don't take a shower in the morning.

Wee-laa Time เวลา

wâang Free/ Available ว่าง	yûng Busy ยุ่ง

PATTERN PRACTICE

yen níi kun wâang mái?	Are you free in this evening?
pŏm yûng mâak, mâi mii wee-laa	I'm so busy, I have no time.
kʉʉn níi chăn wâang rao bpai tîaw dûai-gan ná	I'm free tonight, would you like to go out together?

Seasons

rʉ́-duu Season(formal) ฤดู	nâa Season (informal) หน้า

rɔ́ɔn Hot ร้อน	nǎow Cold หนาว	fǒn Rain ฝน

bai-máai-plì Leaf sprout ใบไม้ผลิ	bai-máai-rûang Leaf fall ใบไม้ร่วง	hì-má Snow หิมะ

Seasons

rʉ́-duu rɔ́ɔn	Summer/Hot season
rʉ́-duu nǎow	Winter/Cold season
rʉ́-duu fǒn	Rainy season
rʉ́-duu bai-máai-plì	Spring
rʉ́-duu bai-máai-rûang	Fall/Autumn

How many seasons in Thailand/your country?

- bprà-têet Thai mii gìi rʉ́-duu? — How many seasons in Thailand?
- bprà-têet kun mii gìi rʉ́-duu? — How many seasons in your country?

There are three seasons in Thailand

- bprà-têet Thai mii 3 rʉ́-duu — There are 3 seasons in Thailand
- mii rʉ́-duu rɔ́ɔn, rʉ́-duu nǎow láe rʉ́-duu fǒn — There is Summer, the Cold season and the Rainy season

PATTERN PRACTICE

chán chɔ̂ɔp dtɔɔn hì-má dtòk	I like it when it snows.
chán mâi chɔ̂ɔp dtɔɔn fǒn dtòk	I don't like it when it's raining.
dʉan nâa fǒn jà dtòk yə́	Next month it will rain a lot.
mʉang Thai mâi mii hì-má	Thailand doesn't have snow.
kun chɔ̂ɔp rʉ́-duu àrai tîi-sùt.	Which season do you like the most?

Weather

aa-gàat bpen yang-ngai
How is the weather
อากาศเป็นยังไง

aa-gàat	The weather / Air
aa-gàat rɔ́ɔn	Hot weather
aa-gàat nǎow	The weather is cold
aa-gàat yen	The weather is cool
aa-gàat dii	The weather is good
aa-gàat mâi dii	The weather isn't good
aa-gàat chʉ́ʉn	It's humid
aa-gàat dtìt lóp	It's minus (x degrees)
aa-gàat bpen-pít	The air polluted

rain/storm/snow

fǒn dtòk	It rains
fǒn dtòk nàk	It rains heavily
fǒn dtòk bprɔɔi bprɔɔi	Light rain
fǒn jà dtòk	It's going to rain
fǒn mâi dtòk	It doesn't rain
fǒn yùt láew	Rain has stopped
mii paa-yú	There's a storm
mii náam tûam	It's flooding
hì-má	Snow
hì-má dtòk	It's snowing

paa-yú hì-má	Blizzard
lom	Wind
lom pát	The wind is blowing
lom raeng	The wind is strong
mii lom pát yen sàbaai	There's a nice breeze

Sunny/Cloudy/Dark

dàed	Sunshine
dàed ɔ̀ɔk	The sun is shining
dàed rɔ́ɔn	The sun is hot (today)
mii mêek mâak	Cloudy
mêek fǒn	Rain cloud
mʉ̂ʉt	Dark
sà-wàang	Bright
mii mɔ̀ɔk nǎa	It's foggy
mii mɔ̀ɔk baang	It's misty

Telling time in Thai is a bit complicated. The time in Thai is very different from English. In Thailand the 24 hour day is divided into segments and uses the familiar 24 hour military time system to some extent. Time is also divided into formal and informal language. The formal time unit is called **na-li-gaa,** which numbers from 0-24 in accordance with international standard time. Informal units change depending on the time of the day.

gìi mong What time is it? **กี่โมง**

Mong O'clock **โมง**	na-lí-gaa O'clock/Watch/Clock **นาฬิกา**

chûa-mong Hour **ชั่วโมง**	naa-tii Minute **นาที**	wí-naa-tii Second **วินาที**

krʉ̂ng Half **ครึ่ง**

PATTERN PRACTICE

ɔ̌ɔ-tôot dtɔɔn-níi gìi mong?	Excuse me, what time is it now?
kun bpai tam-ngaan gìi-mong?	What time do you go to work?
wan-níi rao mii bprà-chum 1 chûa-mong krʉ̂ng	Today we have a one hour half meeting.

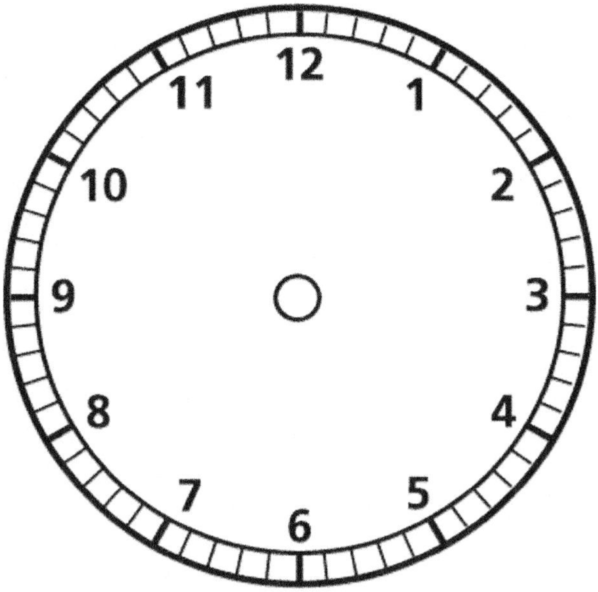

Period of time in Thai

dtɔɔn cháao In the morning ตอนเช้า	dtɔɔn bàai In the afternoon ตอนบ่าย	dtɔɔn yen In the evening ตอนเย็น

dtɔɔn kâm In late evening ตอนค่ำ	dtɔɔn dʉ̀k Late at night ตอนดึก

Thai clock

The Thai way of telling the time originated from the temples and in the past it was the duty of temple staff or monks to inform people of the time. In the past this was the duty of temples. They used the same system as the West where the bell of the church tells everybody the time so that people are able to know time for their daily activities.

Thai use 3 different instrumental sounds for telling the time. That's why there are three different words for telling the time in Thai; "**moong**, **tûm** and **dtii**". There are three different sounds, from three different musical instruments to tell the time for different periods of the day.

The quietest sound, "dtii" is made by hitting a plaque which is only used at night time because it isn't too loud so as to not bother people who are still sleeping. It is used for telling the time from 1 to 5 am.

The loudest sound is used for the majority of the day and it sounds like "moong." During the daytime the temple would use a Thai musical instrument, called a kɔ̂ɔng, to send a signal by hitting it. The sound of the Khong is "moong."

The second loudest bell made a sound like "tûm." After sunset at 6 pm the temple changed to hit the Thai drum called a glɔɔng. The sound of a glɔɔng is "dtûm." That is why the word tûm is used for this time.

A.M.

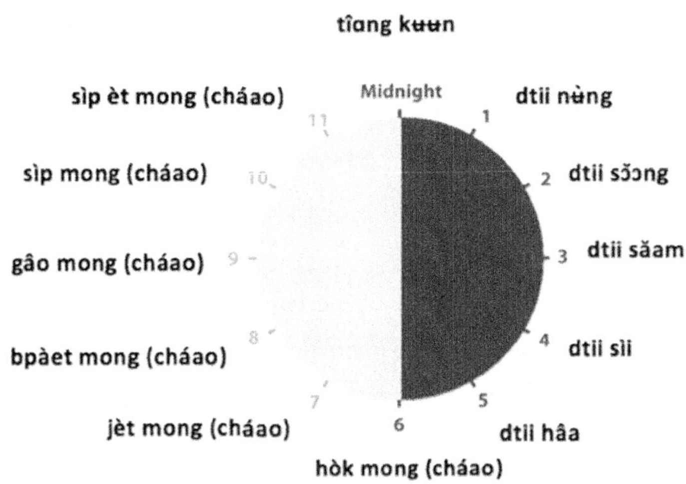

Dtii...	...mong cháao	tîang wan
Time between 1am - 5am	Time between 6am-11am	Mid day
ตี	โมงเช้า	เที่ยงวัน

For telling the time from **1am to 5am**, the number of the hour is preceded by the word **dtii**

dtii nʉ̀ng	1 am
dtii sŏng	2 am
dtii sǎam	3 am
dtii sìi	4 am
dtii hâa	5 am

From **6am to 11am**, the number of the hour is followed by the word **mong** (o'clock) and optionally also **cháao** (morning).

hòk mong (cháao)	6 am
jèt mong (cháao)	7 am
bpàet mong (cháao)	8 am
gâo mong (cháao)	9 am
sìp mong (cháao)	10 am
sìp èt mong (cháao)	11 am
tîang wan	12 pm

P.M.

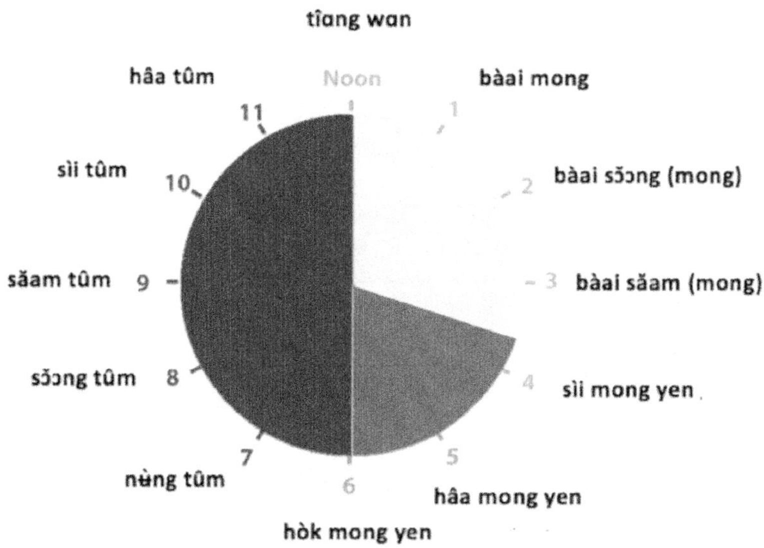

bàai... mong	...mong yen	...tûm	tîang kʉʉn
Between 1- 3pm	Between 4- 6pm	Between 7- 11pm	Midnight

The hours from **1pm to 3pm** are referred to using the words bàai ("early afternoon")

bàai mong	1 pm
bàai sŏng (mong)	2 pm
bàai săam (mong)	3 pm

Yen means evening ("late afternoon/early evening"). 4pm is borderline between the two time-periods and can be referred to using either of them, though it's more common to use **yen.**

sìi mong yen / bàai sèe (mong)	4 pm
hâa mong yen	5 pm
hòk mong yen	6 pm

The hours from 7pm to 11pm are referred to using the numbers 1 - 5 followed by the word tûm.

nʉ̀ng tûm / tûm nʉ̀ng	7 pm
sŏng tûm	8 pm
săam tûm	9 pm
sìi tûm	10 pm
hâa tûm	11 pm
tîang kʉʉn	12 am

Midnight is occasionally referred to as **hòk tûm** but much more common is tîang kʉʉn

Daily activities

6 mong cháao	dtʉ̀ʉn nɔɔn	Wake up
6 mong 15 naa-tii	àab-náam	Take a shower
6 mong 30 naa-tii	dtàeng-dtua	Get dressed
7 mong dtrong	gin aahǎan cháao	Eat breakfast
7 mong krʉ̂ng	bpai rong-rian	Go to school
8 momg dtrong	bpai tam-ngaan	Go to work
10 momg	bpai ráan gaa-fae	Go to coffee shop
tîang	gin aahǎan tîang	Eat lunch
bàai mong krʉ̂ng	rian paa-sǎa Anggrìt	Study English
bàai 3	rian/tam-ngaan sèt	Finish study/work
4 mong yen	bpai sʉ́ʉ-kɔ̌ɔng	Go shopping
5 mong krʉ̂ng	jàai kâa náam	Pay water bill
5 mong 45 naa-tii	glàp bâan	Go home
6 mong yen	tam aahǎan	Cook
6 mong krʉ̂ng	gin aahǎan-yen	Dinner
1 tûm	tam gaan-bâan	Do homework
1 tûm krʉ̂ng	duu Tv gàp krɔ̂ɔp-krua	Watch TV with family
2 tûm	àan nǎng-sʉ̌ʉ	Read books
3 tûm krʉ̂ng	àab-náam/bpraeng-fan	Take a shower/ brush teeth
4 tûm	kâao-nɔɔn	Go to bed

Practice for time

PM

Practice for time

AM

LESSON 8

Family

In Asian and especially Thai Culture the family is very strictly hierarchical. Thais have big families and stay together in a big house or live nearby. Family is the most important thing for a Thai and we have to respect our elders. Watch the way Thai people behave and interact with the elderly and you will see this all the time.

There is no social security or pension system in Thailand unless you are a government employee like a teacher or policeman. Instead, the family fills the role of old age security.

Hierarchy

Traditional Thai society is organized around hierarchy. Hierarchy is based on age, occupation, wealth and residence and the family's financial influence.

Gender/age

pûu-yǐng Lady ผู้หญิง	pûu-chaai Man ผู้ชาย

dèk (pûu)-yǐng Girl เด็กผู้หญิง	dèk (pûu)-chaai Boy เด็กผู้ชาย

wai-rûn Teenager วัยรุ่น

sǎao Young lady สาว	nùm Young man หนุ่ม

pûu-yài Adult ผู้ใหญ่	kon gàe Old people คนแก่	fàràng Westerner ฝรั่ง	lûuk-krʉ̂ng Child of two ethnic groups ลูกครึ่ง

PATTERN PRACTICE

pûu-chaai fàràng lɔ̂ɔ	Western men are handsome.
wai-rûn fàràng mii kwam-mân-jai sǔung	Western teenagers are highly confident.
kon gàe tîi bprà-têet Thai mâi ngǎao	Old people in Thailand never feel lonely.
káo bpen lûuk-krʉ̂ng Thai-America	He is half Thai, half American.

Family

Mii Have มี	krɔ̂ɔp-krua Family ครอบครัว

pɔ̂ɔ Father พ่อ	mâe Mother แม่	Lûuk Child ลูก

pan-rá-yaa (mia) Wife ภรรยา (เมีย)	sǎa-mii(pǔa) Husband สามี (ผัว)

PATTERN PRACTICE

krɔ̂ɔp-krua kun mii krai bâang?	Who is in your family?
krɔ̂ɔp-krua pǒm mii pɔ̂ɔ gàp mâe	My family has my dad and mum
mâe chán yùu tîi America	My mum is in America.
pǒm yùu gàp pan-rá-yaa láe Lûuk	I live with my wife and child.
mii pîi-nɔ́ɔng gìi kon?	How many siblings do you have?

When you first meet people in Thailand they will probably ask about your family. This is normal in Thailand. Don't feel strange if they ask personal questions like: "Have you married yet?" How many children do you have?" or "where is your family?"

You might be asked "mii pîi-nɔ́ɔng gìi kon?" "How many siblings do you have?"

rʉ́-yang
Have......yet?
รึยัง

rian-jòb	dt<u>àe</u>ng-ngaan	tam-ngaan	f<u>ae</u>n
Graduate	Marry	Work	Boyfriend/Girlfriend
เรียนจบ	**แต่งงาน**	**ทำงาน**	**แฟน**

PATTERN PRACTICE

rian-jòb rʉ́-yang?	Have you graduated yet?
mii faen rʉ́-yang?	Do you have a girlfriend/boyfriend?
tam-ngaan tîi-nǎi?	Where do you work?
mii lûuk rʉ́-yang?	Do you have any children?
tam-ngaan rʉ́-yang?	Do you have a job yet?

Note: Popular questions from Thais

The phrase rʉ́-yang is use to ask whether one has done something yet.

yang mâi	l<u>áe</u>w
Not yet	Already
ยังไม่	**แล้ว**

PATTERN PRACTICE

Have you married yet?

Q: kun dt<u>àe</u>ng-ngaan rʉ́-yang?	Are you married yet?
A1: yang	Not yet.
A2: yang mâi dt<u>àe</u>ng-ngaan	Not married yet.
A3: dt<u>àe</u>ng-ngaan l<u>áe</u>w	Married already.

Have you had any children?

Q: kun mii lûuk rʉ́-yang?	Do you have any children?
A1: mii l<u>áe</u>w	(I) already have (children).
A2: yang mâi mii lûuk	(I) Don't have any kids yet.

pîi	nɔ̂ɔng	sǎao	chaai
Older people	Younger people	Young lady	Man
พี่	น้อง	สาว	ชาย

Because the hierachical system is so important and strict in Thailand. When talking to other people you need to put their position before their name.
pîl (older people) and nɔ̂ɔng (younger people) you will hear this a lot in Thailand.

You can use pîi or nɔ̂ɔng followed by the name. Or just pîi / nɔ̂ɔng alone. Used for both male and female.

Example

pîi Jenny	Sister Jenny (elder)
nɔ̂ɔng Eve	Sister Eve (younger)

pîi-nɔ̂ɔng
Sibling
พี่น้อง

pîi- sǎao	nɔ̂ɔng -sǎao
Elder sister	Younger sister
พี่สาว	น้องสาว

pîi-chaai	nɔ̂ɔng-chaai
Elder brother	Younger brother
พี่ชาย	น้องชาย

lûuk-sǎao	lûuk-chaai
Daughter	Son
ลูกสาว	ลูกชาย

PATTERN PRACTICE

lûuk-sǎao 2 kon kɔ̌ɔng kun Tom nâa-rák mâak	Tom's 2 daughters are so cute.
pîi-chaai paa mâe bpai-tîaw	(our) Elder brother is taking mum travelling.
nɔ́ɔng-chaai kɔ̌ɔng pǒm mâi chɔ̂ɔp bpai rong-rian	My younger brother doesn't like going to school.
chán mii pîi-sǎao 1 kon. káo rian tîi chiangmai	I have one Elder sister, she is studying in Chiangmai.

Conversation1

A:	kun mii pîi- nɔ́ɔng mái?	Do you have any siblings?
B:	mii k. chán mii nɔ́ɔng-sǎao 1 kon.	Yes, I have one younger sister
B:	kun là?	What about you?
A:	chán bpen lûuk-kon-diaw .	I'm an only child,
	chán yàak mii pîi- nɔ́ɔng.	I want to have siblings
B:	chán kít-wâa bpen lûuk-kon-diaw	I think being an only child.
	sà-nùk gwàa.	Is more fun.
A:	jing lə̌?	Really?
B:	jing .	Really.

Conversation2

A:	chán yàak mii lûuk mâak.	I really want to have a child.
B:	jing lə̌? tam-mai?	Really? Why?
A:	prɔ́-wâa chán ngǎao.	Because I'm lonely.
B:	kun yàak mii lûuk-chaai rʉ̌ʉ lûuk-sǎao?	Do you want to have a boy or a girl?
A:	táng-sɔ̌ɔng.	Both.

Thai families are divided into 2 sides. Father's side and Mother's side.

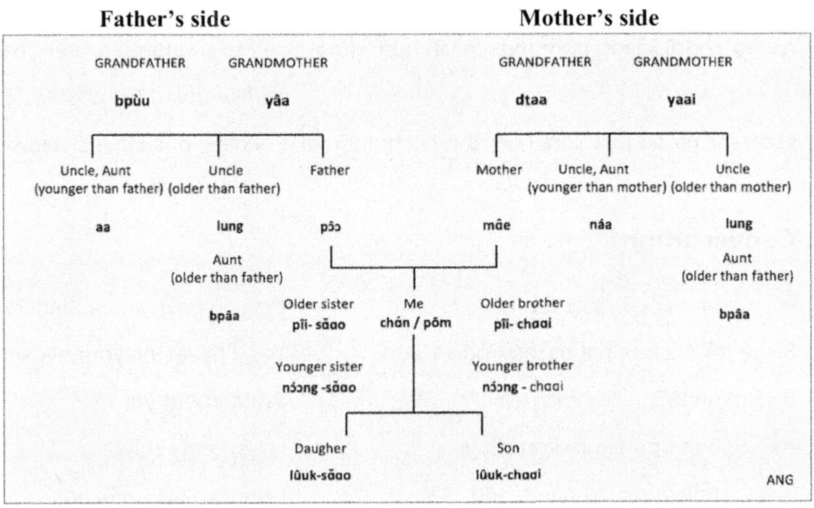

Family member

pɔ̂ɔ	Father	พ่อ
mâe	Mother	แม่
lûuk	Child, Offspring	ลูก
bpùu	Father's father	ปู่
yâa	Father's mother	ย่า
dtaa	Mother's father	ตา
yaai	Mother's mother	ยาย
lung	Uncle (older brother of your mother or father)	ลุง
bpâa	Aunt (older sister of your mother and father)	ป้า
náa	Uncle, Aunt (younger brother or sister on mother's side)	น้า

aa	Uncle, Aunt (younger brother or sister on father's side)	อา
lǎan	Grand children	หลาน
lǎan chaai	Nephew, Grandson	หลานชาย
lǎan sǎao	Niece, Granddaughter	หลานสาว
lûuk pîi lûuk nɔ́ɔng	Cousin	ลูกพี่ลูกน้อง

Thai in-laws

pɔ̂ɔ dtaa	Father-in-law of man	พ่อตา
mâe-yaai	Mother-in-law of man	แม่ยาย
pɔ̂ɔ sǎa-mii	Father-in-law of woman	พ่อสามี
mâe sǎa-mii	Mother-in-law of man	แม่สามี
lûuk kǎəi	Son-in-law	ลูกเขย
lûuk sà-pái	Daughter-in-law	ลูกสะใภ้
pɔ̂ɔ líang	Step father	พ่อเลี้ยง
mâe líang	Step mother	แม่เลี้ยง
lûuk líang	Step child	ลูกเลี้ยง

Everybody seems related to each other

Thai people use the familiar language of relationship with people that they're not related to. For example they will call their friends mother and father pɔ̂ɔ/ mɑ̂e

pîi For both men and women who are older than you

nɔ́ɔng For both men and women who are younger than you

lung For men the age of your uncle

bpâa For women the age of your aunt

náa For women and men younger than your aunt or uncle

dtaa For men the age of your grandfather

yaai For women the age of your grandmother

If you have a Thai friend and they are introducing their 5th set of grandparents or brother and sister, it's better to automatically assume that they are probably not a real relative.

Husband and Wife

There are formal and informal words for husband and wife. The formal word for wife is **pan-ra-yaa.** Informal is **mia.** The formal word for husband is **sǎa-mii** and informal is **pǔa**. It's better to use the formal one.

pan-ra-yaa / sǎa-mii.

If a man has a mistress, she is called "**mia nɔ́ɔi**" and "**mia lǔang**" is used for his official wife.

Boyfriend and girlfriend

Boyfriends and girlfriends are referred to as **faen.** Sometimes you will hear Thais call their wives or husbands as **faen** as well. Though mostly we use this term for couples who are not yet married. If your boyfriend or girlfriend has a secret relationship with someone else, we refer to that person as a **gíg.** This means casual boyfriend/girlfriend or intimate friend.

Sugar papa

sìa/ bpǎa

Sugar mama

jée

Age

Asking for somebodies age in Thailand is very simple and also part of good social etiquette. Don't be offended if asked and don't be afraid of offending, because for Thais if you are talking to someone they will use different words for people who are older or younger. We need to know so we can address you properly and with respect.

aa-yú Age อายุ	gà-sǐan Retired เกษียณ

PATTERN PRACTICE

How old are you?

aa-yú tâo-rài? — How old are you?

aa-yú gìi bpii? — How many years old are you?

I'm ...years old

aa-yú yə̂ — I'm old (quite old).

pǒm aa-yú 23 bpii — I'm 23 years old.

mâe chán aa-yú 50 bpii — My mum is 50 years old.

pɔ̂ɔ pǒm gà-sǐan láew — My dad is retired already.

> kùap = years old (for children, up to the age of 12)
> sòot - single

The elderly will never be lonely in Thailand.

In Thai culture, you are expected to treat the elderly with respect. This is especially ture with regards to your own family, taking care of them is not an option, but a duty. This is a strong tradition in Thailand with roots from Buddhist beliefs.

There is no social security or pension system in Thailand like in western countries unless you are a government employee such as a teacher or policeman. Instead the family fills the role of old age security. That is why you will see Thai people go back to their hometown during the holiday.

1) Greet elders with a wai.

2) Do not stand over or sit above an elder.

3) Speak in a quiet and respectful voice.

4) Never interrupt elders and show respect towards elderly friends and relatives.

5) Spend time with them.

6) Always remember your manners.

Match the words

1......pɔ̂ɔ

2......pan-ra-yaa

3......lûuk

4......yâa

5......mâe

6......dtaa

7......sǎa-mii

8......bpùu

9......lǎan sǎao

10....lung

11....faen

12....náa

13....yaai

14....aa

15....lǎan

16....bpâa

17....lǎan chaai

18....lûuk pîi lûuk nɔ́ɔng

A: Father

B: Mother

C: Child, offspring

D: Father's father

E: Father's mother

F: Mother's father

G: Mother's mother

H: Uncle (older brother of your mother or father)

J: Aunt (older sister of your mother or father)

L: Uncle, Aunt (younger brother or sister on mother's side)

M: Uncle, Aunt (younger brother or sister on father's side)

N: Grandchildren

O: Nephew, Grandson

P: Niece, Granddaughter

Q: Cousin

R: Boyfriend or girlfriend

S: Wife

T: Husband

Let's translate

1.pɔ̂ɔ chán maa jàak bprà-têt Jiin

....

2.mâe mii pʉ̂an yə́

....

3.lûuk

....

4.bpùu mâi chɔ̂ɔp gin gaa-fae

....

5.yaai chɔ̂ɔp bpai wát

....

6.lung yang mâi dtàeng-ngaan

....

7.bpâa mâi mii lûuk

....

8.chán yàak mii lûuk 2 kon

....

9.aa sòot

....

10.bpùu rák lǎan

....

11.lûuk-pîi-lûuk-nɔ́ɔng kɔ̌ɔng chán nâa-rák mâak

....

Answers

1. A
2. S
3. C
4. E
5. B
6. F
7. T
8. D
9. P
10. H
11. R
12. L
13. G
14. M
15. N
16. J
17. O
18. Q

Answers

1. My dad comes from China.
2. Mum has a lot of friends.
3. Children
4. Grandfather (father's side) doesn't like to drink coffee.
5. Grandmum (mother's side) likes to go to the temple.
6. Uncle is not married yet.
7. Aunt doesn't have a baby.
8. I want to have two kids.
9. Uncle, Aunt (younger brother or sister on mother's side) is single.
10. Grandfather (father's side) loves his grandchildren.
11. My cousin is so cute.

LESSON 9

Occupation

aa-chîip	tam-ngaan
Occupation	To work
อาชีพ	ทำงาน

PATTERN PRACTICE

What do you do?

kun tam aa-chîip àrai? — What is your profession?

kun tam-ngaan àrai? — What is your job?

bpen To be เป็น

kruu Teacher ครู	prá Monk พระ	mɔ̌ɔ Doctor หมอ

PATTERN PRACTICE

I am……

chán bpen kruu	I'm a teacher
pǒm bpen prá	I'm a monk
pǒm bpen mɔ̌ɔ	I'm a doctor

yàak bpen Want to be อยากเป็น

PATTERN PRACTICE

dtɔɔn dèk kun yàak bpen àrai?	When you were a kid. What did you want to be?
chán yàak bpen mɔ̌ɔ	I want to be a doctor

Workplace

tîi-tam-ngaan Workplace ที่ทำงาน

bɔɔ-rí-sàt Company บริษัท	roong-ngaan Factory โรงงาน	ùu Garage อู่	awf-fít Office ออฟฟิต

Where do you work?

PATTERN PRACTICE

Where do you work?

kun tam-ngaan tîi-nǎi?	Where do you work?

I work at....

pǒm tam-ngaan tîi bɔɔ-rí-sàt.	I work for a company.
pǒm tam-ngaan tîi roong-ngaan	I work at a factory.
awf-fít pǒm yùu tîi Siam centre	My office is in Siam Centre.
tîi-tam-ngaan pǒm yùu mâi glai	My workplace is not far.

Prefixes for occupation

Three prefixes in Thai are used before the names of occupations. These are "**nák**" "**kon**" "**châang** ".

These can be added to verbs to make those verbs nouns in dictating professions.

nák

nák means "**a person who**"

nák + **VERB / NOUN**

The prefix, "nák" is used for many occupations. We use this word as a prefix with the name of the occupation. For example: business person, writers, accountants, students etc.

nák-rɔ́ɔng Singer นักร้อง	nák-rian Student นักเรียน	nák-sʉ̀k-sǎa University student นักศึกษา

nák-don-dtrii Musician นักดนตรี	nák-túrágìt Business person นักธุรกิจ	nák-gii-laa Athlete นักกีฬา

nák-ɔ̀ɔk-bàeb Designer นักออกแบบ	nák-bin Pilot นักบิน	nák-kǐan Writer นักเขียน

Châang

"**châang**" means an **artisan** and is mostly used with professions involving certain skills e.g. mechanics, barbers, tailors etc. This word refers to a mechanic.

châang dtàt-pǒm	châang fai-fáa	châang dtàt-sʉ̂a
Barber	Electrician	Tailor
ช่างตัดผม	**ช่างไฟฟ้า**	**ช่างตัดเสื้อ**

châang sɔ̂ɔm-rót	châang sɔ̂ɔm-ae	châang-máai
Mechanic	Aircon repairman	Carpenter
ช่างซ่อมรถ	**ช่างซ่อมแอร์**	**ช่างไม้**

kon

"**kon"** means person or people with blue collar professions like drivers, butchers, vendors etc.

kon + VERB +

kon sǔan	kon ngaan	kon tam-kwam-sààat
Gardener	Worker	Cleaner
คนสวน	**คนงาน**	**คนทำความสะอาด**

kon chái	kon kǎai lottery
Maid	Lottery ticket seller
คนใช้	**คนขายล๊อตเตอรี่**

Official Government

In Thailand, most Thais aspire to work as a civil servant because of the social welfare benefits. Fields of Social Welfare which include Education, Health Care, Income Maintainance, Housing and Safety in Life and Property are considered better than other occupations and are also good for families. These jobs are have a very slow career path and a small income but have stability. In Thailand not every job will get pension, only the civil servant occupations below get a pension.

kâa-râat-cha-gaan
Civil servant
ข้าราชการ

tá-hǎan	aa-jaan	dtam-rùat
Soldier	Professor	Police
ทหาร	**อาจารย์**	**ตำรวจ**

gà-sǐan
Retired
เกษียณ

ngən bam-naan	ngən bam-nèt
Pension	Pension/Retirement allow ance
เงินบำนาญ	**เงินบำเหน็จ**

PATTERN PRACTICE

kâa-râat-cha-gaan bpen aa-chîip tîi dii	Civil servant is a good job.
chán yàak bpen aa-jaan	I want to be a professor.
kun pɔ̂ɔ-kun mâe chán gà-sǐan láew	My parents are retired already.
kon Thai mâi mii ngən- bam-naan	Thai people have no pension.

White collar

jâo-kɔ̌ɔng	lee-kǎa
Owner	Secretary
เจ้าของ	เลขา

pûu-jàt-gaan	pá-nák-ngaan	hǔa-nâa
Manager	Staff/Officer	Boss
ผู้จัดการ	พนักงาน	หัวหน้า

PATTERN PRACTICE

jâo-kɔ̌ɔng mâi yùu tîi-nîi — The owner is not here.
pá-nák-ngaan maa sǎai bɔ̀ɔi bɔ̀ɔi — The staff come late very often.
hǔa-nâa jai-dii — The boss is so kind.
pûu-jàt-gaan mâi chɔ̂ɔp dʉ̀ʉm gaa-fae — The manager doesn't like to drink coffee.

tam-ngaan-ìtsàrà
Freelancer
ทำงานอิสระ

prá	mâe-bâan	chaao-naa
Monk	Housewife	Farmer
พระ	แม่บ้าน	ชาวนา

chaao-sǔan	pɔ̂ɔ káa/mâe káa	Joon/kà-moi
Gardener	Merchant/Retailer	Thief/Robber
ชาวสวน	พ่อค้า แม่ค้า	โจร ขโมย

daa-raa Movie star ดารา	wít-sà-wá-gɔɔn Engineer วิศวกร	gáai Tour guide ไกด์

Use verbs to describe

tam-ngaan hâi... Work for... ทำงานให้

kàp-rót Drive car ขับรถ	sɔ̌ɔn nǎng-sʉ̌ʉ Teaching สอนหนังสือ	kǎai-kɔ̌ɔng Sell things ขายของ

PATTERN PRACTICE

pǒm tam-ngaan hâi kun Peter	I work for Peter.
pǒm kàp-rót tîi Roong-ngaan	I drive for the factory.
chán kǎai-kɔ̌ɔng tîi dtà-làat	I sell things at the market
chán sɔ̌ɔn tîi Rong-rian	I teach at the school.

Salary

ngən-dʉan	kâa-jâang	raai-jàai
Salary	Wage	Expenditure
เงินเดือน	ค่าจ้าง	รายจ่าย

PATTERN PRACTICE

Chiangmai ngən-dʉan mâi yə́ — In Chiangmai the salary isn't high.

tam-ngaan kâa-jâang wan lá 300 baht — Wage is 300 baht per day.

dʉan níi raai-jàai yə́ mâak — This month we have a lot of expenditures.

jâang	lâi-ɔ̀ɔk	sà-màk-ngaan	hǎa-ngaan
Hire	To fire	To apply job	To hunt job
จ้าง	ไล่ออก	สมัครงาน	หางาน

PATTERN PRACTICE

pɔ̂ɔ jâang kon sǔan 1 kon — Dad hires one gardener.

káo tùuk lâi-ɔ̀ɔk jàak ngaan — He was fired from work.

prûng-níi chán jà bpai sà-màk-ngaan — Tomorrow I'll go and apply for a job.

kun khuan hǎa-ngaan — You should be looking for work.

mâi mii ngaan tam No work to do ไม่มีงานทำ	dtòk-ngaan To be unemployed ตกงาน

PATTERN PRACTICE

pîi-chaai mâi mii ngaan tam	My big brother has no job.
mâi mii krai yàak dtòk-ngaan	No one wants to be unemployed.

To know

rúu To have knowledge/Know information รู้	rúu-jàk To know people/Places/Things รู้จัก

The difference between the words "**rúu**" and "**rúu-jàk**". Simply put, the word "**rúu**" refers to something that is knowledge. For instance, you know how to speak Thai.

The word "**rúu-jàk**" refers to being aware of the "existence" of something. For instance, you know of the existence of the Thai language.

English doesn't have this differentiation as when speaking English, you always use the word know and can infer its meaning from the context of the sentence.

PATTERN PRACTICE

chán rúu wâa káo mâi chɔ̂ɔp chán	I know that he doesn't like me.
pǒm rúu wâa kun chɔ̂ɔp aa-hǎan tá-lee	I know that you like seafood.
pǒm rúu-jàk kun Jan	I know Ms. Jan.
kun rúu-jàk kâao-nǐaw-má-mûang mái?	Do you know the Thai sweet sticky rice with mango?

LESSON 10

Adjective

Noun + Adjective

yài	lék	gào	mài
Big	Small	Old (things)	New
ใหญ่	เล็ก	เก่า	ใหม่

nàk	bao	kǣng-rǣng	ɔ̀ɔn-ae
Heavy	Light	Strong	Weak
หนัก	เบา	แข็งแรง	อ่อนแอ

an-dtà-raai	bplɔ̀ɔt-pai	sà-àat	sòk-gà-pròk
Dangerous	Safe	Clean	Dirty
อันตราย	ปลอดภัย	สะอาด	สกปรก

PATTERN PRACTICE

bâan yài	Big house.
chán mii mǎa lék	I have a small dog.
too-rà-sàp gào	Old telephone.
yàak sʉ́ʉ sʉ̂a mài	Want to buy a new shirt.

Describing people

uân	pɔ̌ɔm	sǔung	dtîa
Fat	Thin	Tall/high(height)	Short(height)
อ้วน	ผอม	สูง	เตี้ย

sân	yaao	chà-làat	ngôo
Short	Long	Smart	Stupid
สั้น	ยาว	ฉลาด	โง่

ruai	Jon	nâa-glìat	sǔai
Rich	Poor	Ugly	Beautiful
รวย	จน	น่าเกลียด	สวย

PATTERN PRACTICE

pûu-yǐng uân	Fat lady.
pǒm kít-wâa pûu-yǐng Thai sǔai	I think Thai girls are beautiful.
fà-ràng sǔung	Tall westerner.
kruu Ang ruai mâak	Teacher Ang is so rich.

Thai Comparatives

gwàa
Than
กว่า

gwàa means more, more than. Inequality more (than), comparing the differences between two things or two people

PATTERN PRACTICE

tá-lee sǔay- gwàa puu-kǎao mâak	The sea is much more beautiful than the mountains.
aa-hǎan thai pèt gwàa aa-hǎan fàràng	Thai food is more spicy than western food.
dii- gwàa	To be better than.

kʉ̂n Up or to increase ขึ้น	long Less or decrease ลง

Talking about changes in one thing, one person or a certain group of things or people.

PATTERN PRACTICE

sŭai- kʉ̂n	To be more beautiful (than before).
pŏm rúu-sʉ̀k dii-kʉ̂n	I feel better.
kun pûut paa-săa angrìt gèng kʉ̂n	You speak English better.

Exercise

a. kʉ̂n

b. long

c. gwàa

Exercise

kun pûut paa-săa Thai gèng ____ bpii tîi láew

fà-ràng sŭung ___ kon Thai

kun mâi sàbaai dtɔɔn-níi dii___ mái

paa-săa Angrìt kɔ̌ɔng chán yâe ___ prɔ́ mâi fʉ̀k.

Grungtêp rɔ́ɔn ____ Chiangmai jing-rɔ̌ɔ?

Characteristics and personality

sǔai Beautiful สวย	râa-rəng Cheerful ร่าเริง	nâa-rák Cute น่ารัก	bâa Crazy บ้า

lɔ̀ɔ Handsome หล่อ	kà-yǎn Diligent ขยัน	kîi-nǐaw Stingy ขี้เหนียว	kîi-gìat Lazy ขี้เกียจ

jai-dii Kind/Nice ใจดี	jai-dam Unkind/Mean ใจดำ	jai-yen Clam/Patient ใจเย็น	jai-rɔ́ɔn Impatient ใจร้อน

PATTERN PRACTICE

káo sǔai mâak	You are so beautiful.
káo bpen kon nâa-rák	He is a lovely person.
kun Pat kà-yǎn tam-ngaan	Pat works hard.
bpâa kîi-nǐaw mâak	Aunt is so stingy.
kun Robert jai-dii mâak	Robert is so kind.

Jai words

jai words are words that describe characteristics;
hŭa-jai this is the physical organ in your chest. In Thai, the word "jai" is a noun and also means "heart" or "mind".

The word heart is also associated with a spiritual use and is used to describe feelings or characteristics. In the Thai language there are literally hundreds of **jai** words.

jai is used as prefix and suffix.

Prefix

The word jai is combined with other words to create the feeling of the emotion described.

jai-dii	Kind	ใจดี
jai-dam	Mean	ใจดำ
jai-rɔ́ɔn	Impatient	ใจร้อน
jai-yen	Calm	ใจเย็น
jai-glâa	Bold	ใจกล้า
jai-gwâang	Generous	ใจกว้าง
jai-ráai	Cruel	ใจร้าย
jai-ɔ̀ɔn	Submissive	ใจอ่อน
jai-ngâai	Naive/Credulous	ใจง่าย
jai-kǎeng	Adamant	ใจแข็ง

Suffix

Words that describe emotions or feelings generally end with jai.

dii-jai	Glad	ดีใจ
kâao-jai	To understand	เข้าใจ
chʉ̂a-jai	To trust	เชื่อใจ
greng-jai	To be considerate	เกรงใจ
nâe-jai	To be certain	แน่ใจ
puum-jai	Proud	ภูมิใจ
sŏn-jai	Interested	สนใจ
tùuk-jai	To be pleased	ถูกใจ
jing-jai	To be sincere	จริงใจ
hĕn-jai	To sympathize	เห็นใจ
bplìan-jai	Change mind	เปลี่ยนใจ
dtâng-jai	Intend	ตั้งใจ
sà-baai-jai	Be happy/Feel content	สบายใจ
bplàek-jai	To be surprised	แปลกใจ
sĭa-jai	Sad	เสียใจ

Common words for characteristics and personality

nâa-bʉa	Boring	น่าเบื่อ
glâa-hǎan	Brave	กล้าหาญ
rɔ̂ɔp-kɔ̂ɔp	Careful	รอบคอบ
bprà-màat	Careless	ประมาท
mii-sànè	Charming	มีเสน่ห์
chà-làat	Clever	ฉลาด
mân-jai	Confident	มั่นใจ
jâao-lê	Crafty/ Tricky	เจ้าเล่ห์
sàbaai-sàbaai	Easy going	สบาย ๆ
mii chʉ̂ʉ-sǐang	Famous	มีชื่อเสียง
kîi-lʉʉm	Forgetful	ขี้ลืม
bpen-gan-eng	Friendly	เป็นกันเอง
yâe	Horrible	แย่
hěn-gàe-dtua	Selfish	เห็นแก่ตัว
kîi-ngɔɔn	Touchy/Peevish	ขี้งอน
nâa-glìat	Ugly	น่าเกลียด
an-dtà-raai	Dangerous	อันตราย
mii kwam-kít sâang-sǎan	Creative	มีความคิดสร้างสรรค์
nâa-sǒn-jai	Interesting	น่าสนใจ

What's he/she like?

bpen kon yang-ngai?
What's he/she like?
เป็นคนยังไง

PATTERN PRACTICE
what's he/she like?

kun Dave bpen kon yang-ngai?	What's Dave like?
káo bpen kon yang-ngai?	What's he/she like?

He/she is....

kun Dave jai-dii mâak láe kà-yǎn tam-ngaan	Dave is so kind and works hard.
káo bpen-gan-eng láe mii-sànè	She is so friendly and charming.
káo lɔ̀ɔ dtàe jâao-chúu	He is handsome but flirtatious.
pɔ̂ɔ jai-rɔ́ɔn mâak	Dad is so impatient.
káo chɔ̂ɔp pûut sǐang-dang	He likes to speak loudly.

Being loud in public
sǐang-dang
It is considered impolite. Be aware of the volume of your voice. It is basically impolite to shout, yell, or speak loudly in public. Talk at a normal volume instead of shouting.

kîi word

Actually, the word "kîi" means excrement or dung and can also function as a noun meaning "feces." However, in the Thai language we use this word as a "prefix" to describe negative personality traits of a person.

Functioning as a prefix it is used with many adjectives and verbs in order to create adjectives used for describing the characteristics, the qualities and the traits that make up someone's personality. These personality traits are mostly negative.

kîi+ adjective/ verb
Negative Personality Traits of Someone

Here are some interesting examples:

kîi-lʉʉm	To be forgetful	ขี้ลืม
kîi-mao	An alcoholic person	ขี้เมา
kîi-niǎw	To be stingy	ขี้เหนียว
kîi-giàt	To be lazy	ขี้เกียจ
kîi-aai	Is shy/ Is timid	ขี้อาย

kîi-móo	Is boastful	ขี้โม้
kîi-goo-hòk	Is dishonest	ขี้โกหก
kîi-uàt	To be show off / Bragging	ขี้อวด
kîi-glua	To be a coward	ขี้กลัว
kîi-ìt-chǎa	Is jealous	ขี้อิจฉา
kîi-hʉ̌ng	Is Jealous (of a relationship)	ขี้หึง
kîi-lên	Playful/ Is a joker	ขี้เล่น
kîi-goong	Is sly/ Is cunning	ขี้โกง

PATTERN PRACTICE

káo bpen kon kîi-lʉʉm	He is a forgetful person.
pûu-chaai kon nán káo kîi-uàt	That guy is very showy.
káo kîi-mao mâak mâak	He is an alcoholic.
káo bpen khon kîi-niǎw	She is a stingy person.
yàa bpen kon kîi-glua	Don't be a coward.
Wan-níi pǒm kîi-giàt ɔ̀ɔk bpai khâang-nɔ̂ɔk	I am too lazy to go out today.

Prefix word "**nâa**"

nâa

Worth ...

น่า

In the Thai language, the word "**nâa**" is a prefix.
(worth v+ing, -able, -ing) + Verb or Adjectives, this prefix turns a verb into an adjective which expresses an opinion of the verb as "worth doing" similar to the "-able" suffix in English and it also has a lot of different meanings.

Thai adjective words with the prefix "nâa"

nâa-rák	Cute, Lovely	น่ารัก
nâa gin	Delicious, Appetising	น่ากิน
nâa - àan	Worth reading	น่าอ่าน
nâa -bpai	Worth going to	น่าไป
nâa -glua	Frightening	น่ากลัว
nâa -gliàt	Ugly, Hateable	น่าเกลียด
nâa -yùu	Cozy, Livable	น่าอยู่
nâa - sʉ́ʉ	Worth buying	น่าซื้อ
nâa -sŏng- săan	Pitiful	น่าสงสาร
nâa- chʉ̂ʉ	Believable	น่าเชื่อ
nâa -sŏn-jai	Interesting	น่าสนใจ
nâa -lɔɔng	Worth trying	น่าลอง
nâa - wái-jai	Trust worthy	น่าไว้ใจ
nâa - ram-kaan	Annoying	น่ารำคาญ
nâa - náp-tʉ̌ʉ	Worthy of respect	น่านับถือ
nâa - sŏng-săi	Suspicious	น่าสงสัย
nâa -bʉ̀a	Boring	น่าเบื่อ

PATTERN PRACTICE

lûuk-mǎa nâa-rák mâak	The puppy is so cute.
aa-hǎan Thai nâa-gin	Thai food is so appetising.
pûu-yǐng kon nán nâa-rák mâak	That lady/girl is so cute.
nǎng pǐi nâa-glua mâak	Ghost movies are very scary.
nǎng rʉ̂ang níi nâa-duu jang-ləəi	This movie is really worth watching.
mʉang Chiang-Mai nâa-yùu mâak	Chiang Mai city is a pleasant place (to live).

Feeling

in Thailand, it is not polite to show emotions in public. Thais are especially offended when one openly displays anger.

gròot	Angry	โกรธ
glua	Afraid	กลัว
dtʉ̀ʉn-dtên	Excited	ตื่นเต้น
aai	Shy	อาย
sǐa-jai	Sad	เสียใจ
bʉ̀a	Bored	เบื่อ
bpen-hùang	Compassion/Be anxious	เป็นห่วง
mân-jai	Confident	มั่นใจ
pìt-wǎng	Disappointed	ผิดหวัง
nʉ̀ai	Tired	เหนื่อย
ìt-chǎa	Jealous	อิจฉา
ngǎao	Lonely	เหงา
dii-jai	Glad	ดีใจ
krîat	Stressed	เครียด
ʉ̀t-àat	Uncomfortable	อึดอัด
dtòk-jai	Frightened	ตกใจ
jai-yen	Patient	ใจเย็น
ngoong	Confused	งง

LESSON 11

Parts of the body

Body parts

râang-gaai	Body (formal)	ร่างกาย
dtua	Body (common)	ตัว
hǔa	Head	หัว
pǒm	Hair (head only)	ผม
nâa	Face	หน้า
dtaa	Eyes	ตา
jà-mùuk	Nose	จมูก
bpàak	Mouth	ปาก
hǔu	Ears	หู
kɔɔ	Neck	คอ
lài	Shoulder	ไหล่
òk	Chest	อก
kǎen	Arms	แขน
mʉʉ	Hands	มือ
kɔ̂ɔ-sɔ̀ɔk	Elbow	ข้อศอก
nom	Breasts	นม
tɔ́ɔng	Stomach	ท้อง
gôn	Bottom/Bum	ก้น
kǎa	Legs	ขา
táao	Feet	เท้า

níw	Finger; Toe; Digit	นิ้ว
kàao	knees	เข่า
níw mʉʉ	Fingers	นิ้วมือ
níw táao	Toes	นิ้วเท้า
kǒn	Hair (body)	ขน
nùat	Mustache	หนวด
krao	Beard	เครา
pǐw	Skin	ผิว
lǎng	Back	หลัง

Body parts are worthy of different levels of respect.

Don't Touch the Head

The head is considered the most important part of the body. You should never touch anyone's head. Except for a child's but you should refrain from this unless the child is in your extended family and a bond has already been established.

Hands and fingers

Don't Point! Pointing at someone is considered rude in many cultures especially in Thailand. Don't use one finger to point, it's rude. Pointing at inanimate objects and animals is acceptable but it's more polite to point with your entire hand rather than a single finger. When motioning for someone to come over bend your hand downwards with your fingers leaning toward the floor and your palm facing upward and also never point at anything with your feet.

To call a taxi or a person, signal them with a palm down, hand waving action. Do not use your index finger to call someone or to point somewhere or at somebody.

Passing Items

Tossing or pushing with the foot is an impolite way to pass something. When passing something, use your right hand because your left hand is used for passing unsanitary things in the bathroom.

The foot

The foot is the lowest part of the body and is also considered to be "dirty". Never point your foot at someone or raise your feet higher than someone's head. When sitting, try to sit in a way that doesn't show your feet. Do not sit with your legs extended out in front of you. Also avoid stepping over people who are sitting or sleeping on the ground.

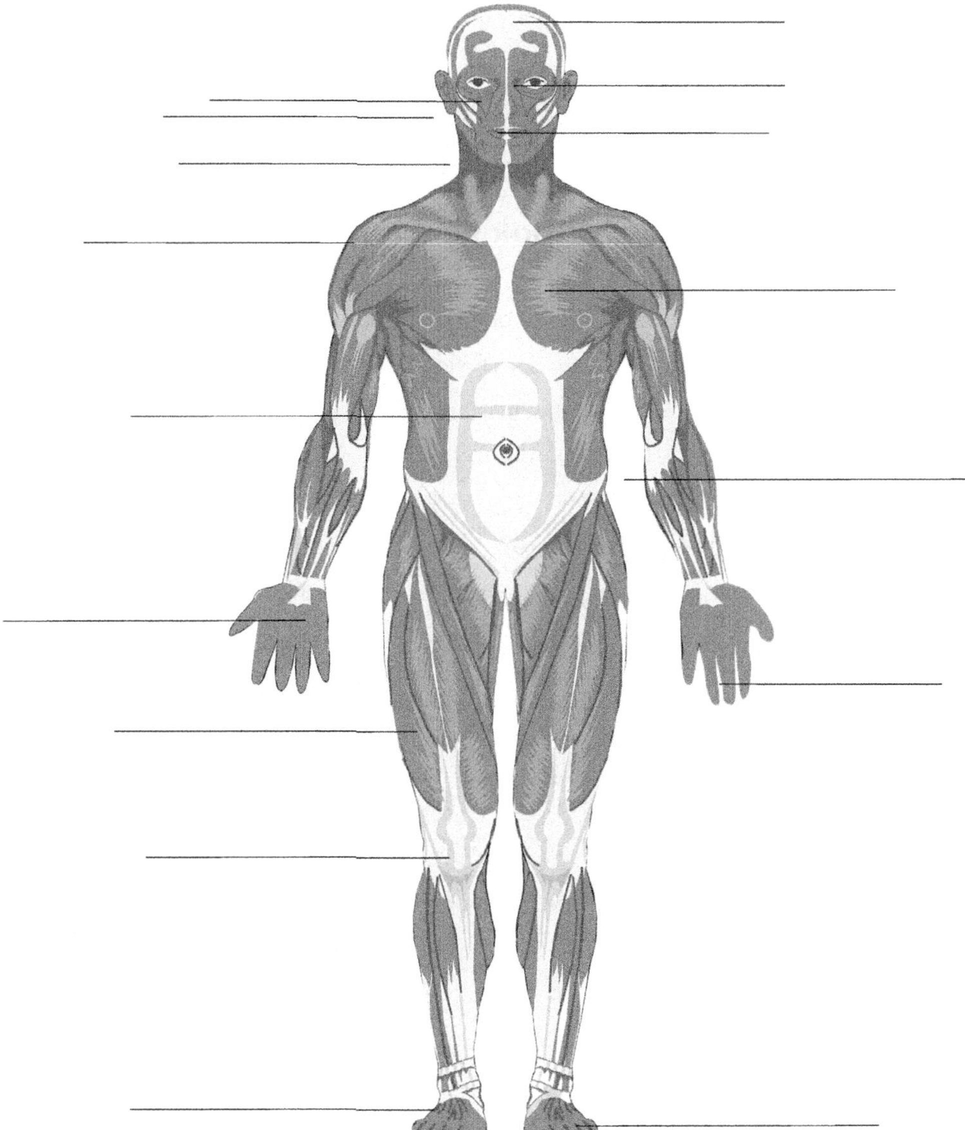

What does he/she look like?

nâa-dtaa bpen yang-ngai?

How does he look like?

หน้าตาเป็นยังไง

PATTERN PRACTICE

What does he/she look like?

kun Eve nâa-dtaa bpen yang-ngai?	What does Eve look like?
kun Robert nâa-dtaa bpen yang-ngai?	What does Robert look like?

He/she is....

kun Eve duu mʉ̌an kon jiin	Eve looks Chinese.
kun Robert sǔung láe uân	Robert is tall and fat.
káo pɔ̌ɔm mâak	He is so skinny.
kun Mike mii pǒm yaao láe pǐw kǎao	Mike has long hair and white skin.

Sickness

bpen àrai?
What's wrong?
เป็นอะไร

mâi sà-baai	bpùai
Not well/Not comfortable	Sick, ill
ไม่สบาย	ป่วย

PATTERN PRACTICE

chán mâi sà-baai bɔ̀ɔi bɔ̀ɔi	I'm sick often.
pǒm bpùai 3 wan láew	I've been sick for 3 days.
tâa mâi yàak bpùai dtɔ̂ɔng ɔ̀ɔk-gam-lang-gaai túk-wan	If you don't want to get sick you should exercise everyday.
pʉ̂an mâi maa rong-rian prɔ́-wâa mâi sà-baai	My Friend didn't come to school because he/she is sick.

bpen wàt	bpen kâi	bpen má-reng
Get a cold	Get a fever	Get cancer
เป็นหวัด	เป็นไข้	เป็นมะเร็ง

PATTERN PRACTICE

káo bpen wàt prɔ́-wâa aa-gàat nǎow	He caught a cold because of the cold weather.
lûuk-sǎao bpen kâi	(my) Daughter has a fever.
bpen má-reng tɔɔ-rá-maan mâak	(I) Have cancer so I'm suffering.
bpen wàt lá-gɔ̂ɔ mii nám-mûuk	(I) Have a cold and a runny nose.

How do you feel?

rúu-sʉ̀k yang-ngai?
How do you feel?
รู้สึกยังไง

jèb	bpùat	mʉ̂ai
Hurt	Pain	Aching/Feel stiff
เจ็บ	ปวด	เมื่อย

PATTERN PRACTICE

chán rúu-sʉ̀k mâi sà-baai	I feel unwell.
chán jèb kǎa prɔ́-wâa mǎa gàt	My leg hurts because a dog bit me.
bpùat hǔa prɔ́ mâi sà-baai	I have a headache because I'm sick.
mʉ̂ai kǎa prɔ́ dəən yə́ gəən-bpai	My legs ache from walking too much.
kun Bryan bpùat tɔ́ɔng prɔ́ gin aahǎan mâi sà-àat	Bryan has a stomach ache because he ate dirty food.

Symptoms

uâk/aajian	wien-hǔa
Vomit	Dizzy
อ้วก/อาเจียน	เวียนหัว

jaam	ai	kan	pǽe
Sneeze	Cough	Ichy	Allergic
จาม	ไอ	คัน	แพ้

PATTERN PRACTICE

káo jaam prɔ́-wâa bpen-wàt	He sneezed because he has a cold.
kun Eve ai láe jèb kɔɔ	Eve has a cough and sore thoat.
kan mâak prɔ́ yung gàt	So itchy from a mosquito bite.
chán páe aa-hǎan tá-lee	I'm allergic to seafood.

hàk

Broken

หัก

PATTERN PRACTICE

chán mâi kəəi kǎen hàk	I've never broken my arm.
fan hàk prɔ́-wâa dtòk gâo-îi	I broke tooth because of falling from a chair.
kɔ̂ɔ-táao hàk prɔ́ lên fóot-bɔɔn	I broke ankle from playing football.
òk hàk prɔ́ faen mii gíg	I broken heart because my boyfriend has hide lover.

sùk-kà-paâp Health สุขภาพ

kǎeng-raeng Strong แข็งแรง	ɔ̀ɔn-ae Weak อ่อนแอ

PATTERN PRACTICE

pɔ̂ɔ kǎeng-raeng mâak	Dad is so strong.
tâa ɔ̀ɔn-ae jà mâi sàbaai bɔ̀ɔi	If you are weak you will get sick frequently.
túk kon yàak sùk-kà-pâap dii	Everyone wants to be healthy.

dii kʉ̂n Get better ดีขึ้น	hǎai Recover หาย

yaa Medicine ยา	dtrùat To check ตรวจ	chìit-yaa To inject ฉีดยา	pák-pɔ̀ɔn Take a rest พักผ่อน

PATTERN PRACTICE

dii kʉ̂n rʉ́-yang?	Feel better or not?
hǎai láew	Recovered already.
kun dtɔ̂ɔng bpai dtrùat râang-gaai	You need to get a check up.
chán pák-pɔ̀ɔn	I'm taking a rest.
bpai-hǎa mɔ̌ɔ	Go to see a doctor.
gin yaa	Take medicine.

Sickness

aa-hǎan bpen-pít	Food Poisoning	อาหารเป็นพิษ
rôok grà-prɔ́	Gastritis	โรคกระเพราะ
rôok kâi lʉ̂at ɔ̀ɔk	Dengue Fever	โรคไข้เลือดออก
tɔ́ɔng sǐa	Diarrhea	ท้องเสีย
mai gren	Migraine	ไมเกรน
rôok bao-wǎan	Diabetes	โรคเบาหวาน
rôok eed	Aids	โรคเอดส์
rôok kwam-dan loo-hìt sǔung	Hypertension	โรคความดันโลหิตสูง

Name of medicine

yaa gâe bpùat	Pain killer	ยาแก้ปวด
yaa gâe ai	Cough medicine	ยาแก้ไอ
yaa gâe kâi	Fever medication	ยาแก้ไข้
yaa gâe páe	Allergy medication	ยาแก้แพ้
yaa kum	Birth control pills	ยาคุม
yaa mɔ̀ɔng	Tiger balm	ยาหม่อง
yaa dom	Nasal Spray	ยาดม
yaa sà-mǔn-prai	Herb	ยาสมุนไพร
yaa taa	Gel/Cream	ยาทา
yaa nɔɔn-làp	Sleeping pills	ยานอนหลับ
yaa wít-dtaa-min	Vitamin	ยาวิตตามิน
bpláat-tə̂ə	Bandaid/ Plaster	พลาสเตอร์
pâa-pan-plǎe	Bandage	ผ้าพันแผล

hǎai reo reo	hǎai wai wai
Get well soon	Get well soon
หายเร็ว ๆ	หายไว ๆ

PATTERN PRACTICE

hǎai reo reo ná	Get well soon.
hǎai wai wai ná	Get well soon.

Useful expression when sick

kun duu mâi dii ləəi	You don't look very well.
kun bpen àrai mái?	Are you ok?
aa-gaan bpen yang-ngai?	What are your symptoms?
wǎi mái?	Can you do it? (even though you're sick).
gin yaa rʉ́-yang	Have you taken any medicine yet?
dii kʉ̂n rʉ́-yang?	Do you feel better yet?
hǎai rʉ́-yang?	Have you recovered yet?
rúu-sʉ̀k yang-ngai?	How do you feel?
chán mâi-kɔ̂ɔi sà-baai	I'm not well.
pák-pɔ̀ɔn yə́ yə́ ná	Take a rest.

The use of particles

In Thai, there are words that have no specific meaning that are used to show the speaker's opinion, attitude or feeling towards the thing they are talking about.

ná นะ is used as a confirmative particle and in most cases, is equivalent to "okay?"
Example

rɔɔ sàk krûu ná ká	Please wait a moment, okay?
prûng-níi chán bpai gàp pʉ̂an ná	Tomorrow I will go with my friend, ok?
rao bpai gin kâao dûai-gan ná	Let's go eat together, ok?
tâa yàak gin àrai bɔ̀ɔk pǒm ná	If you want to eat anything, tell me, ok?

sì สิ/ซิ is used to express enthusiasm or encouragement. It is generally used in imperative.

Example:

rian Thai dtɔ̂ɔng pûut paa-sǎa Thai sì	Study Thai must speak Thai!
yàa tam bàeb nán sì	Don't do it like that!
tâa hǐw dtɔ̂ɔng gin sì	If you are hungry you must eat!
kâo-jai pǒm nɔ̀ɔi sì	Please understand me!

dâi sì kŕap/ká is a phrase used as a positive response to questions.

Example:

A: prûng-níi bpai yîam mâe dûai-gan mái?	Tomorrow would you like to go visit mum together?
B: dâi sì ká.	That would be great.
A: chûai bpai-sòng pǒm tîi bâan dâi-mái?	Can you help to take me home?
B: dâi sì ká, mâi mii bpan-hǎa	Of course, No problem.

Emergency

chûai dûai! Help! ช่วยด้วย	chûai To help ช่วย

ù-bàt-dtì-hèt Accident อุบัติเหตุ	lǒng taang Get lost หลงทาง	bàat- jèb Get injured บาดเจ็บ

PATTERN PRACTICE

chûai dûai! chán lǒng taang — Help! I'm lost.

mii kon bàat-jèb 2 kon — Two people were injured.

tîi-nân mii ù-bàt-dtì-hèt bɔ̀ɔi — Over there have accidents often.

rót rong-pà-yaa-baan Ambulance รถโรงพยาบาล	rót chùk-chə̌ən Ambulance รถฉุกเฉิน	bəə chùk-chə̌ən Emergency call number เบอร์ฉุกเฉิน

PATTERN PRACTICE

chûai too-rîak rót rong-pà-yaa-baan — Help! Call the ambulance.

rót chùk-chə̌ən yang mâi maa — The Ambulance still hasn't come.

Emergency situations

mii rót chon gan	Have a car crash	มีรถชนกัน
mii kon jèb	Some people were injured	มีคนเจ็บ
mii kon dtaai	Someone has died	มีคนตาย
mii kon tà-lɔ́ gan	Some people is fighting	มีคนทะเลาะกัน
káo mii bpʉʉn	He has a gun	เขามีปืน
káo mii yaa-bâa	He has methamphetamines	เขามียาบ้า
mii fai-mâi	There's a fire	มีไฟไหม้
mii ù-bàt-dtì-hèt	Have an accident	มีอุบัติเหตุ
mii kà-mooi	There's a thief	มีขโมย
kɔ̌ɔng hǎai	Things were stolen	ของหาย
bplôn tá-naa-kaan	Bank robbery	ปล้นธนาคาร

Hâam Forbid ห้าม	Yàa Do not อย่า

PATTERN PRACTICE

tâa mâi sàbaai hâam bpai rong-rian	If (you're) sick, don't go to school.
yàa nɔɔn-dʉ̀k	Don't go to bed late.
yàa dʉʉm lâao yə́	Don't drink too much alcohol.
tâa bpùat tɔ́ɔng hâam gin aahǎan pèt	If you have a stomatch ache, don't eat spicy food.

Visa

Wii-sâa Visa วีซ่า

kɔ̌ɔ Asking for ขอ	Dtɔ̀ɔ Extend ต่อ	Mòt aa-yú Expired หมดอายุ

PATTERN PRACTICE

kun mii vii-sâa àrai?	What kind of visa do you have?
kɔ̌ɔ vii-sâa	Ask for a visa.
dtɔ̀ɔ vii-sâa	Extend your visa.
vii-sâa mòt aa-yú	Visa expired.

Type of visa

Tourist visa	wii-sâa nák-tɔ̂ɔng-tîaw
Retirement visa	wii-sâa gà-sǐan
Education visa	wii-sâa nák-rian
Marriage visa	wii-sâa dtàeng-ngaan
Working visa	wii-sâa tam-ngaan
Volunteer visa	wii-sâa aa-sǎa-sà-màk

Useful words

Passport	páat-pɔ̀ɔt
Document	èk-gà-sǎan
Immigration	dtɔɔ-mɔɔ
To wait	rɔɔ
Copy	tàai èk-gà-sǎan
Queue up	kâo kiw
Line up	kâo tǎew
Picture	rûup-tàai
Address	tîi-yùu
Information	kɔ̂ɔ-muun

dtɔ̂ɔng	khuan
Must/Have to	Should
ต้อง	**ควร**

PATTERN PRACTICE

kun dtɔ̂ɔng gin aahǎan yə́ yə́	You have to eat a lot.
chán dtɔ̂ɔng bpai tam-ngaan	I have to go to work.
kun mâi khuan sùup bù-rìi	You shouldn't smoke.
kun khuan bpai gàp káo	You should go with him.

LESSON 12

Transportations

Vehicle

rót-fai-fáa	Sky train	รถไฟฟ้า
rót-fai-dtâi-din	Subway	รถไฟใต้ดิน
rót-bát/rót-mee	City bus	รถบัส รถเมล์
rót-tua	Overnight bus	รถทัวร์
sǎam-lɔ́ɔ	Tricycle	สามล้อ
dtúk-dtúk	Tricycle taxi	ตุ๊กตุ๊ก
rót-t<u>áe</u>k- sîi	Taxi	แท็กซี่
sɔ̌ɔng-t<u>ǎe</u>w	Two row mini bus	สองแถว

......yang-ngai?
How
ยังไง

rót(yon)	jàk-grà-yaan	krʉ̂ang-bin
Car	Bicycle	Airplane
รถ(ยนต์)	จักรยาน	เครื่องบิน

rʉa	mɔɔ-dtəə-sai	rót-fai
Boat	Motorcycle	Train
เรือ	มอเตอร์ไซค์	รถไฟ

PATTERN PRACTICE

How did you come/go....?

kun maa tîi-nîi yang-ngai? How did you get here?

kun bpai Rong-rian yang-ngai? How do you go to school?

bpàk-gà-dtì kun bpai tam-ngaan yang-ngai? Normally how do you go to work?

bpai dtà-làat yang-ngai? How do I go to the market?

kìi To ride ขี่	kàp To drive ขับ

nâng To sit (as a passenger) นั่ง	bpai (dooi) Go by means of.... ไปโดย

PATTERN PRACTICE

kun kìi jàk-grà-yaan dâi mái?	Can you ride a bicycle?
chán yàak lɔɔng kìi cháng.	I want to try riding an elephant.
chán kàp rót bpai tam-ngaan	I drive to work.
pǒm nâng táek-sîi maa tîi-nîi	I came here by taxi.
káo bpai America dooi krʉ̂ang-bin	He goes to America by plane.

long Get off ลง	kʉ̂n Get on ขึ้น

PATTERN PRACTICE

kun dtɔ̂ɔng long tîi bpâai-rót nâa	You need to get off at the next bus station.
chán kʉ̂n krʉ̂ang-bin láew	I'm already on the airplane.
kʉ̂n rót tîi-nân	Get in that car.
kʉ̂n krʉ̂ang-bin dǐaw-níi	Get on the airplane right now.

bpai sòng Go and take to ไปส่ง	maa sòng Come and take to มาส่ง

bpai ráp Go to pick up ไปรับ	maa ráp Come to pick up มารับ

PATTERN PRACTICE

túk wan chán bpai-sòng mâe tîi-tam-ngaan	Everyday I take mum to work.
wan níi faen maa-sòng	Today my boyfriend took me here.
chuâi bpai-ráp kun Jame nɔ̀ɔi	Can you help go pick up Jame?
maa-ráp tîi bâan ná	Come pick me up at home.

ɔ̀ɔk To leave ออก	tʉ̌ng To arrive ถึง

PATTERN PRACTICE

rót-mee ɔ̀ɔk bprà-maan 8 mong	The bus will leave around 8 am.
chán jà tʉ̌ng Chiangmai prûng-níi	I'll arrive in Chiangmai tomorrow.
Kun jà tʉ̌ng chiangmai mʉ̂a-rài?	When will you arrive in Chiangmai?
chán ɔ̀ɔk bâan sǎai	I leave home late.

chái wee-laa
Spend time
ใช้เวลา

chái which means "to use" and Wee-laa means "time"

PATTERN PRACTICE

chái wee-laa gìi chûa-mong?	How many hours will It take?
rian paa-sǎa Thai dtɔ̂ɔng chái wee-laa	Studying Thai takes time.
chái wee-laa naan	It takes a long time.
jàak tîi-nîi bpai sà-nǎam-bin chái wee-laa naan mái?	From here to the airport it takes a long time?

dtrong-weelaa	sǎai
On time	Late
ตรงเวลา	**สาย**

PATTERN PRACTICE

kon yîi-bpùn dtrong-weelaa sàmə̌ə	Japanese are always on time.
chán bpai rong-rian sǎai sàmə̌ə	I always go to school late.

Useful words

To book	jɔɔng
To rent	châo
To cancel	yók-lôək
To board	kʉ̂n krʉ̂ang
Pass through	pàan
To park	jɔ̀ɔt
To check in	chék in
Hurry	rîip
Traffic jam	rót dtìt
Delay	lâa-cháa
Bus stop	bpâai-rót mee
Ticket	dtŭa
Insurance	bprà-gan
Journey	gaan-dəən-taang
Business	tú-rá-gìt
Passenger	pûu dooi săan
Fare	kâa dooi săan
Price	raa-kaa
Map	păen-tîi
Tax	paa-sĭl
Round trip	bpai-glàp
One way trip	tîaw diaw
Tourist	nák tɔ̂ɔng-tîaw
Travel agency	bɔɔ-rí-sàt Tour
Side walk	taang-táao

Example sentence

chûai jɔ̀ɔt nâa bɔɔ-rí-sàt	Please stop in front of the company.
pǒm yàak châo rót	I want to rent a car.
pǒm kɔ̌ɔ yók-lêək dtǔa	I want to cancel the ticket.
kʉ̂n krʉ̂ang gìi-mong	What time is boarding?
rót-mee níi pàan sà-nǎam-bin mái?	Will this bus pass through the airport?
rîip nɔ̀ɔi	Hurry up.
rót-dtìt túk-wan nâa-bʉ̀a mâak	Traffic jams everyday are so boring.
krʉ̂ang-bin lâa-cháa 1 chûa-mong	Flight is delayed for 1 hour.

Money

ngən Money (common) เงิน	dtang Money (spoken lanuage) ตังค์

lâek To exchange แลก	oon Transfer โอน	tɔ̌ɔn Withdraw ถอน	fàak Deposit ฝาก

PATTERN PRACTICE

lâek ngən dâi tîi-nǎi?	Where can I exchange money?
chán yàak oon ngən hâi mâe	I want to transfer money for mum.
tɔ̌ɔn ngən tîi dtûu-ATM	Withdraw money at the ATM.
kun khuan fàak ngən túk dʉan	You should deposit money every month.

jàai Pay จ่าย

yʉʉm To borrow ยืม	kʉʉn To return คืน

PATTERN PRACTICE

chán mâi yàak yʉʉm ngən pʉ̂an	I don't want to borrow my friend's money.
káo jà kʉʉn ngən wan-níi	He will give me back the money today.
pǒm hâi-yʉʉm nǎng-sʉ̌ʉ	I lent a book.
kɔ̌ɔ yʉʉm too-rà-sàp dâi mái?	Can I borrow your telephone?

ngən mát-jam

Deposit money

เงินมัดจำ

PATTERN PRACTICE

Liza:	jɔɔng hɔ̂ɔng 2 hɔ̂ɔng kâ	I would like to book 2 rooms.
Reception:	chʉ̂ʉ kun àrai ká?	What is your name?
Liza:	chʉ̂ʉ Liza kâ	My name is Lisa.
Reception:	kâ 2 hɔ̂ɔng 2 kʉʉn ná ká?	Ok. 2 rooms for 2 nights?
Liza:	châi kâ	Yes.
Reception:	mii ngən mát-jam	Ok we need 2,000 baht per room.
	hɔ̂ɔng lá 2,000 ná kâ	For a deposit.
Liza:	nîi kâ. táng-mòt 4,000 baht kâ	Here you are. All together 4,000 baht.
Reception:	kun ráp ngən mát-jam kʉʉn wan chék-áot kâ	You can get the deposit back when you check-out.
Liza:	kâ kɔ̀ɔp kun kâ	Thank you.
Reception:	yin dii kâ	You're welcome.

Financial Transactions

tam To do/To make ทำ	bpə̀ət To open เปิด	bpìt To close ปิด

Vocabuary

Bank account	ban-chii tá-naa-kaan
ID card	bàt bprà-chaa-chon
Credit card	bàt credìt
Member card	bàt sà-maa-chík
ATM card	bàt ATM
Bank book	sà-mùt ban-chii tá-naa-kaan
Sign	sen

PATTERN PRACTICE

chán yàak bpə̀ət ban-chii tá-naa-kaan	I want to open a Bank account.
bàt bprà-chaa-chon hǎai	Lost ID card.
yàak yók-lə̂ək bàt credìt	I want to cancel my credit card.
bàt ATM chái mâi dâi	Can't use ATM card.
chûai sen tîi-nîi	Can you sign here?

Bill

kâa Fee/Charge ค่า

kâa náam Water bill ค่าน้ำ	kâa fai Electric bill ค่าไฟ	kâa châo Rental bill ค่าเช่า
kâa internet Internet bill ค่าอินเตอร์เน็ต	kâa rian Tuition ค่าเรียน	kâa kâo Entrance fees ค่าเข้า
kâa rong-raem Hotel expense ค่าโรงแรม	kâa rót Fare ค่ารถ	kâa too-rá-sàp Telephone bill ค่าโทรศัพท์

PATTERN PRACTICE

kâa-kâo mâi paeng ləəi	Entrance fee is not expensive at all.
kâa-rian paa-săa Thai mâi paeng ləəi	Studying Thai is not expensive at all
kâa-rót tùuk mâak	Fare is very cheap.
kâa-châo bâan tîi chiangmai,	House rental in Chiangmai.
bprà-maan 15,000 THB	is around 15,000 baht.

mâi......ləəi

Not at all

ไม่เลย

PATTERN PRACTICE

mâi àrɔ̀ɔi ləəi	Not delicious at all.
mâi chɔ̂ɔp ləəi	Don't like at all.
mâi sǔai ləəi	Not beautiful at all.
mâi ngâai ləəi	Not easy at all.

What you think about Thai language?

I have studied three other languages, but never a tonal language like Thai. I have found learning to hear and produce the correct tones is probably the most difficult thing as I have studied the Thai language, but don't give up! With the guidance of a great teacher, helpful learning resources, and plenty of practice I have found we can learn to speak Thai! Kru Ang has been a wonderful teacher and an outstanding source of understandable and interesting information that not only has helped me begin speaking Thai, but she also has opened a door to learn more about the beautiful culture and people of Thailand.

Von Newcomb
(USA)

Ein neues Highlight auf dem Markt der phonetischen Lehrbücher für die thailändische Sprache. Da macht das Lernen Spaß!

A new highlight on the market for learning the Thai language from the beginning to the intermediate level! It`s a real fun to learn!

Hans Karsten Hartwigsen
(Germany)

Знание тайского языка очень полезно, если Вы собираетесь провести некоторое время в красивой стране улыбок - Таиланде. Язык можно выучить, общаясь с местными, тем самым все ближе познакомиться с красивой тайской культурой.

If you plan to spend some time in Thailand you will definitely need to learn Thai language. It will help you better understand the beautiful Thai culture and people. Learning to read is a little bit difficult, but it gives so many opportunities if you can do it!

Mariam Davtyan
(Russia)

Aprender tailandés es un desafío motivante para mí. Me encanta descubrir la cultura tailandesa y su filosofía de vida a través de su lengua.
El alfabeto y los tonos es lo más difícil de aprender. Por el contrario, la estructura de las frases y los tiempos verbales son muy fáciles.
Los tailandeses siempre me animan y ayudan a aprender más cuando intento hablar en tailandés con ellos.

Learning thai lenguage is a motivating challenge for me. I love to discover thai culture and thai people philosophy of life through their lenguage.
The alphabet and the tones are the most difficult learning areas. By contrast, sentence structure and verbal tenses are very easy.
Thai people always encourage and help me to learn more when I try to speak thai lenguage with them.

blanca Castro
(Spain)

初心者から中級者までのタイ語学習のハイライト。

本当に楽しく学習できます！

Yoshi Ban (Japan)

泰语是一门很有意思的语言，不过，你需要时间去慢慢适应它

Thai is a very interesting language, but you need time to get used to it

Robin Zhuangzi(China)

Si vous prévoyez de partir en Thaïlande juste pour quelque semaine, quelque mois ou plus, le simple fait de connaître quelque mot, Quelque phrase, malgré toutes les difficultés, cinq tons, un nouvel alphabet, de nouvelle sonorité, changera la relation que vous aurez avec les habitants. Difficile oui mais tellement plaisant.

If you planned to go in Thailand just for vacation or for a longer period you will find that just to know a few words, a few sentences, despite all the difficulties of the language, five tones, an all new alphabet, new pronunciations, will change the relationship you'll have with local people. Difficult, yes totally, rewarding, yes totally.

Jerome Vigo (France)

YOU CAN NEVER

UNDERSTAND ONE LANGUAGE

UNTIL

YOU UNDERSTAND

AT LEAST TWO

More information and Skype lesson

Angsiyanan Ounping (Kru Ang)
Facebook: Ang Ang Payne
Angsiyanan@yahoo.com

Printed in Great Britain
by Amazon

14619425R00120